Every Christian needs to read this i
challenges and negative effects of gospels that are devoid of discipleship and
reminds us that salvation includes full life in Christ as we grow to be more
like him.

    —**Robby Gallaty**, *Senior Pastor, Long Hollow Baptist Church;*
president of Replicate Ministries

With biblical and theological precision, *The Discipleship Gospel* instructs us
to replace the gospel of easy believism with Jesus' gospel of the kingdom.
Until we get the gospel right, we can't expect the state of discipleship to
change. This book takes us to the very foundation upon which disciple
making is built.

    —**Greg Ogden**, *author of* Transforming Discipleship; *Chairman of*
the Board, Global Discipleship Initiative

Bill and Ben show us how Jesus' gospel calls us to both salvation and
discipleship—no exceptions, no excuses. I pray that every pastor and leader
who reads it will be changed by it.

    —**Bobby Harrington**, *pastor and cofounder of Discipleship.org*

This is an urgent, essential read for every Christian. The popular version
of the gospel has produced 'cultural Christians,' and this book offers the
remedy—understanding and spreading the full gospel of king Jesus. I pray
its healing medicine is widely distributed.

    —**Larry Walkemeyer**, *pastor and author; Superintendent, Free*
Methodist; Director of Equipping, Exponential

The Discipleship Gospel combines scriptural teaching with entertaining
storytelling to show why the only path to salvation is through discipleship
to Jesus, the forgiving king. A compelling resource for the Church.

    —**Matthew W. Bates**, *author of* Salvation by Allegiance Alone; *Associate Professor of Theology, Quincy University*

THE

DISCIPLESHIP

GOSPEL

WHAT JESUS PREACHED—
WE MUST FOLLOW

Bill Hull & Ben Sobels

To Jane and Joni, who unapologetically live the discipleship gospel with great joy

CONTENTS

INTRODUCTION

"As egg-headed as it may sound, our basic problem is our theology. The problem is our doctrine of salvation."

—DALLAS WILLARD

Why must we define the gospel today? Let's start with a common scene that takes place in the counseling chambers of hundreds of pastors every day. Someone comes to the leader's office and says, "I'm divorcing my mate. I've fallen in love with someone else, and I'm no longer happy. I need to do this."

The pastor protests, "You can't do that—it's wrong! You don't have a good, biblical reason to divorce. If you follow through, you're committing adultery, and whomever you marry will become an adulterer as well."

The person looks at the pastor, almost whimsically, and says, "Of course I can. You've been teaching for years that God will forgive all my sins—that was handled on the cross. All my sins—past, present, and future—are forgiven. I'm going to heaven when I die anyway, so no one can snatch me out of the Father's hand. I am secure in Christ because it's all about grace."

At this juncture, it's "game, set, match" for many church leaders. We've found ourselves in this situation, just as you may have in one way or another.

At this point, we don't have much to say because the person is merely repeating to us what we have taught them. They are misconstruing our teaching, of course, but the damage has already been done. We could try to protest and say, "No, God won't forgive you (at least anytime soon)! That is, unless you repent of your sin, which includes turning away from this new relationship."

But that doesn't work.

Another option is that we could give a convincing presentation about, "reaping what you sow," or about how God's discipline will bear upon them one day, and they will have a long, hard life if they continue on this path. Chances are, though, they will ignore our advice, divorce their spouse, and marry the new person. In a few years though, they'll be serving, teaching, and leading people at another congregation like nothing happened.

You know what happens next, don't you? They ask God to forgive them for the wrong they've done, glorying in the fact that, "God worked all things together for the good." They rejoice in how much happier everyone is—both them and their ex-spouse—and how the children are "just fine."

In my (Bill's) many years of pastoral experience, this scenario is all too common.

That kind of rationalization is possible though because the primary gospel preached in America today, by default, is the "forgiveness-only gospel," which is almost exclusively focused on sin and atonement.[1] The forgiveness-only gospel is connected to the idea of saying a magic prayer that gets you into heaven one day. It's a sort of transaction between the one praying and God, where the person gets a salvation ticket. Behavior in this "gospel" is in no way connected to this initial transaction. As long as your barcode is correct—*beep*—you're allowed into heaven.

This kind of teaching leads people to think they believe the gospel because that's what they've been taught. Over time, the truth is revealed that they did not believe at all; they had simply agreed with a religious proposition. It's an innocent error though because emphasizing forgiveness *is part of the full gospel*. The problem is that they don't really *believe* Christ; they only *profess faith in* Christ. It is a grave error to equate profession of faith with belief. That's why it's important to set the record straight, rebuild our understanding of the gospel, and crack the code of the gospel that Jesus preached—what we're calling the "discipleship gospel."

Our purpose in this project is twofold. First, we introduce the problem with preaching non-discipleship gospels that don't call people to be disciples. As such, these false gospels don't lead people to make disciples. Second, we show that the New Testament gospel writers made very clear to their audience seven essential elements of the gospel Jesus preached. Jesus' gospel led his disciples to make disciples. Please keep in mind that the seven elements do not comprise a definition of the gospel. They do, however, provide the critical framework for defining the gospel, which we explore in this book, too. We must be sure to preach Jesus' gospel, which is a gospel of discipleship. The longer we preach non-discipleship gospels, the more we delay the fulfillment of Christ's great commission.

As you read this book, we offer you a clear definition of Jesus' discipleship gospel. This definition of the gospel, we believe, will help you and those in your church gain crystal clarity on the nature of the gospel so that you can be fully equipped to answer in our day the question, "What is the gospel?"

Toward the end, we'll discuss how Jesus' discipleship gospel can incite a discipleship revolution in your life and create a disciple-making movement in your church and in your world.

PART ONE

THE GOSPEL JESUS PREACHED

In this part of the book, we get into the weeds of the problem as we see it. However, we're spending only enough time on the problem to get to a clear solution. Focusing on the problem can get us tangled into a theological pretzel if we don't continue toward a solution.

The true gospel is Jesus' gospel, which he referred to as the "gospel of the kingdom" (Matt. 24:14), and this gospel was crystal clear to the early church (Acts 2:14-41). Since then though, the church has drifted away from preaching Jesus' gospel—at various times and in different ways—and has believed in different "gospels," which aren't really gospels at all. They all have one common characteristic: they remove the necessity of discipleship from Jesus' gospel. The type of preaching that comes from believing these gospels ultimately suffocates disciple making in the church. Yet making disciples is one of the greatest tasks that Christ has called the church to do until he returns. In our day, the church has once again loosed its mooring from the dock of Jesus' gospel and has been carried away by the currents of our culture—with the wind and the waves—to believe in false gospels.

After describing the problem, we'll lay the foundation for recovering Jesus' gospel for the church. Specifically, we're unpacking the gospel that Jesus preached. While gospel preaching in our day seems so ill-defined and changeable, it was static and well-defined in Jesus' day—so clearly defined that people knew when they had received it, what they had been entrusted with, and when they had passed it on to others (2 Tim. 2:2). The gospel had definition for the early believers, and that is what we seek with this book—to provide a clear definition of the gospel for believers today.

In Part 1, we open up the four Gospel records together—primarily Mark's Gospel—and begin to see just how clearly Jesus defined the gospel. Specifically, we want to show you that the gospel Jesus preached had seven essential elements, which provide the framework on which believers today can rebuild their understanding of Jesus' gospel, the only true gospel—what we call *the discipleship gospel*. As we rediscover this together, the key component of Christ's gospel that we're missing today is this: Christ doesn't call us to make *a decision* about the gospel, but to *be disciples* because of his gospel. With these things in mind, let's jump into this fascinating and critical gospel discussion by first unpacking the nature of the problem so that we can understand the solution with greater precision.

1

THE DISCIPLESHIP GOSPEL
(A.K.A. THE KINGDOM GOSPEL)

"Let the pure gospel go forth in all its lion-like majesty, and it
will soon clear its own way and ease itself of its adversaries."

—CHARLES SPURGEON

New Testament scholars agree that Jesus spoke about the kingdom of
God more than anything else during his earthly ministry—more than
one hundred times in fact.[1] He used many parables and metaphors to explain
the mysteries of the kingdom. But unfortunately, saying that people today
are a bit fuzzy on the meaning of "the gospel of the kingdom" is an under-
statement. Confusion abounds, so let's simplify the meaning here by addressing the essence of what Jesus was asking people to do when he announced the
Good News of the kingdom—namely, to follow him as a disciple.

The way to get a handle on the kingdom and its vast claim over humanity was by repenting of sins, believing in Jesus as the messiah, and following

him as a rabbi.[2] People today also need to repent of their sins, believe the Good News about Jesus as savior, and follow him as teacher and Lord. To join his kingdom, we must become disciples or "apprentices" of Jesus, people who actually do what he did. That is why we are calling the gospel of the kingdom "the discipleship gospel." What we mean is that *"discipleship"—or following Jesus—is an essential part of the Good News he preached.*

The Good News of the kingdom is that eternal life begins now—the moment you repent, believe the Good News of Christ, receive the Holy Spirit, and start following him.[3] Repentance, belief, and Spirit-filled obedience go together. God never intended for them to be separated (as if that were possible). The kingdom is holistic: you enter a new realm where "all things are become new" (2 Cor. 5:17, KJV). When you start following Jesus, you begin to prove you believe what he says. This is quite different from what is commonly taught as the gospel: that if you believe the right religious facts, you're saved, and following Jesus is just an option. What we must teach, however, is that Jesus started with the call to follow him. His disciples started believing in him and grew spiritually in stages. We defy any experienced follower of Jesus who says that growing through a gradual process is not an accurate description of their life in Christ. Life in Christ doesn't begin with instant maturity and immediate understanding; it starts with essential elements and grows from there.

The Place of Obedience

Our deepest desires are revealed by our daily life and habits. The Anglican preacher and evangelist John Wesley had it right when he encouraged the right behaviors among new believers—behaviors that led them to deepen their belief over time. John's Gospel shows us that although the original five disciples began to follow Jesus by faith alone, the other disciples grew in their faith when they witnessed his first miracle of turning water into wine: "This miraculous sign at Cana in Galilee was the first time Jesus revealed his glory. And his disciples believed in him" (John 1:35-51). As the disciples followed the one who had called them, their belief deepened. Simply put, we are believers first, and we deepen our beliefs through the practices, traditions, and habits of our lives.

Don't misunderstand us though. On a certain level, believing produces behavior, too. It must be that way; otherwise, each of us would draw the line of conversion in different places. Only God knows what true belief is—that's why we're not the judges. One thing is clear: following Jesus is an actual, existential behavior that demonstrates the reality of our faith in him (James 2:14-20).[4]

At the heart of the gospel of the kingdom is the simple question, "Are you doing the will of God?" This comes from Jesus' message centering on the vital role of obedience to enter God's kingdom: "Not everyone who calls out to me, 'Lord! Lord!' will enter the Kingdom of Heaven. Only those who actually do the will of my Father in heaven will enter" (Matt. 7:21-23). This passage reveals to us that living in the kingdom is the same as being a disciple of Christ, someone who does the will of God. When you decide to follow Christ, you enter a new realm, a new kingdom, where his will is done. Recall the prayer that Jesus taught his disciples to pray: "May your Kingdom come soon. May your will be done on earth, as it is in heaven" (Matt. 6:10).[5] This passage also shows us that following Jesus is vital to entering the kingdom of God. So even in The Lord's Prayer, Jesus taught his disciples that heaven is where God's will is done and that wherever his will is done on earth, the kingdom exists.

The same is true for us today. We must obey God; otherwise, we don't really understand the gospel Jesus preached. That's why the word "discipleship" is crucial—because we're following a living Christ. We appreciate the sobering words of the twentieth-century German pastor and theologian Dietrich Bonhoeffer who was martyred for his faith: "Christianity without discipleship is always Christianity without Christ."[6] A faith that isn't lived out through action is not faith; it's a life without Christ. Plain and simple, if you want the living Christ, then you must follow him. That is discipleship, and that's why we call it "the discipleship gospel."

What Happened to Following Jesus?

Most of Jesus' apostles were in their late teens and early twenties. They were products of orthodox Jewish homes and local synagogues where they had learned the Scriptures. They were conversant with the great messianic passages from the prophets. From this starting point, Jesus taught them about the kingdom and showed them what it looked like in this world.[7] Because of

The Discipleship Gospel

this, they understood him as king, the promised messiah. They didn't need to work through centuries of Christian tradition to figure out what he wanted.

In fact, the Gospel of Mark includes the call to follow Jesus in Jesus' earliest preaching in Galilee: "The Kingdom of God is near! Repent of your sins and believe the Good News!" (Mark 1:14-15). Then, they took the most logical action possible. They followed him and became his disciples:

> One day as Jesus was walking along the shore of the Sea of Galilee, he saw Simon and his brother Andrew throwing a net into the water, for they fished for a living. Jesus called out to them, "Come, follow me, and I will show you how to fish for people!" And they left their nets at once and followed him.
>
> —MARK 1:16-18

The disciples' response to Jesus' call was directly connected to Jesus' preaching about the kingdom. They heard his message, followed him, and became his disciples.

Connecting Faith to Action

It's impossible to separate belief from action. They are one and the same. When the disciples followed Jesus, they fully made themselves his disciples. They entered into a new realm, and that's when eternal life began for them. They were doing God's will in their lives on earth as it already was in heaven (as The Lord's Prayer says). Jesus began to teach them the importance of seeking first his kingdom:

> Don't worry about these things, saying, "What will we eat? What will we drink? What will we wear?" These things dominate the thoughts of unbelievers, but your heavenly Father already knows all your needs. Seek the Kingdom of God above all else, and live righteously, and he will give you everything you need.
>
> —MATTHEW 6:31-33

For Jesus (and his disciples as they grew in their faith), the kingdom of God was central to eternal life. That's why it was part of the Good News he preached.

Through his many parables, Jesus worked out the implications of the kingdom into every facet of life, yet the full reality of the kingdom was still somewhat of a mystery, even after Jesus' resurrection. Luke's words in Acts 1:6-7 reveal to us: "[The apostles] kept asking him, 'Lord, has the time come for you to free Israel and restore our kingdom?' He replied, 'The Father alone has the authority to set those dates and times, and they are not for you to know.'"

Many a disciple has wanted the kingdom in all its fullness right now. Even Jesus was in the same position as his followers, in a sense, because he didn't know when the kingdom would be fully restored, yet he longed to usher in the kingdom in the present. Luke shares the account of Jesus crying out over Jerusalem:

> O Jerusalem, Jerusalem, the city that kills the prophets and stones God's messengers! How often I have wanted to gather your children together as a hen protects her chicks beneath her wings, but you wouldn't let me. And now, look, your house is abandoned. And you will never see me again until you say, "Blessings on the one who comes in the name of the Lord!"

—Luke 13:34-35

Despite Jesus' cries, his Hebraic world said "no" to the kingdom, and God responded, "Okay, no kingdom for you now, not yet—but I will be back!" The church—comprised of Jews and Gentiles who have become one in Christ—experiences the blessings of the kingdom that Christ inaugurated during his first coming. The apostles themselves were a bit confused about this whole thing, and as we saw above in Acts 1, they asked Jesus for a definitive answer at the very last moment before he ascended.

Where Is the Kingdom of God?

The main thing to remember about kingdom talk is that we don't know many specifics about the kingdom. The restoration of the kingdom referenced in Acts 1:6-7 obviously had something to do with military and political power. The Jews of the time wanted political liberation from the Romans. The apostles asked about the kingdom restoration even though none of them could remember a time when Israel was free from the Roman yoke. Jesus' message of the kingdom fulfilled their longings, but not in the ways they expected.

Jesus not only led people into the kingdom; he also showed them what it looked like. He explained it to the general populace and demonstrated it daily in his teachings and works. When Jesus arrived at his hometown of Nazareth, for example, he went to the synagogue and made his announcement in a straightforward and startling way. He began by reading from the Isaiah scroll:

> "The Spirit of the Lord is upon me, for he has anointed me to bring Good News to the poor. He has sent me to proclaim that captives will be released, that the blind will see, that the oppressed will be set free, and that the time of the Lord's favor has come." He rolled up the scroll, handed it back to the attendant and sat down. All eyes in the synagogue looked at him intently. Then he began to speak to them. The scripture you've just heard has been fulfilled this very day!
>
> —LUKE 4:16-21

Jesus' fellow Nazarenes in the synagogue seemed to appreciate his words. In fact, they were amazed that a young man from such humble origins could be so bright, so professional. Jesus, however, was a contrarian by nature. Other rabbis would have taken in the accolades and ended there, but not Jesus. He knew them too well—he knew their pride and their prejudice. So he pressed into their unspoken criticism: "You will undoubtedly quote me this proverb: 'Physician, heal yourself'—meaning, 'Do miracles here in your hometown like those you did in Capernaum.' But I tell you the truth, no prophet is accepted in his own hometown" (Luke 4:23-24).

Of course, this statement alone wasn't what got under the skin of the city fathers; his historical reference about prejudice sparked their ire:

> Certainly there were many needy widows in Israel in Elijah's time, when the heavens were closed for three and a half years, and severe famine devastated the land. Yet Elijah was not sent to any of them. He was sent instead to a foreigner—a widow of Zarephath in the land of Sidon. And there were many lepers in Israel in the time of the prophet Elisha, but the only one healed was Naaman, a Syrian.
>
> —LUKE 4:25-27

This Scripture passage implies that the citizens of Nazareth will not see the miracles in their village because they will not honor its native son as the anointed one, the messiah. They will only get a small bit of the good that could have been theirs through humility and faith. Jesus was saying to them, "God will send me, the Son of God, to other places, where minds are open and hearts prepared." His accusation angered them: "When they heard this, the people in the synagogue were furious" (Luke 4:28-30).

Luke's account reveals that people easily rejected Jesus and his kingdom, but the kingdom of God is where God's will is done. Jesus told the disciples that God would send him to other places, even—and maybe especially— to Gentile regions. He would, as Elijah and Elisha did, bless the unwashed and despised Syrians because they were more open to God than the Jews.[8] God's will could not be done in Nazareth; it could, however, be done in other places—more unlikely places. Those unlikely places were the land of the unwashed, the half-breeds, and outcasts.

Discipleship Isn't Optional

The contemporary church is quite human and behaves very much like Jesus' fellow Nazarenes. The kingdom of God has had as much trouble getting underway in the contemporary church as it did when Jesus did great work in his hometown. The citizens of Nazareth couldn't see beyond the boy Jesus to the messiah Jesus. They were so prejudiced against God showing any favor to any group other than them that they were ready to kill him. As humans, we tend to take the blessings of the gospel—which should lead us to receiving Christ's love and sharing it with others—and instead hoard them selfishly (even violently!) for ourselves. Doing this distorts the gospel from being others-focused to being self-focused.

The church's greatest barrier toward thriving today is that she believes in distortions of the gospel. This comes, in part, because of what we preach (and what we leave out of our preaching). The most common gospel preached in the developed world—in places like the United States, Canada, Western Europe, parts of Africa and Asia, Australia, and New Zealand—is the forgiveness-only, consumer gospel. The problem with this gospel is that it's only part of the truth.

Gospel Distortions

Many of those in the developing world, however, don't quite have it down either. In our experience, the most common gospel in underdeveloped countries is the prosperity gospel, which makes discipleship almost impossible to teach as an essential part of the Good News. This kind of gospel turns everyone into a consumer of religious goods and services.

Neither version—neither the forgiveness-only gospel nor the prosperity gospel—includes discipleship as a normative part of what it means to be saved. Both gospels make no room for the ways and means of the kingdom that Jesus

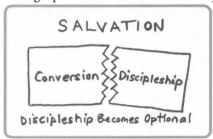

passed on to his followers. Neither has a serious connection to character transformation, and neither really expects everyone who is "saved" to actually follow Jesus. Moreover, these "gospels" don't set the precedent for making disciples who make disciples. The idea that every believer in Christ is a follower of Christ is not a common part of the theology, programs, or curricula of these churches.[9] In other words, both of these gospels have a fatal flaw—they separate conversion from discipleship, thus making discipleship optional.

Through our work with The Bonhoeffer Project, a community of people and resources bent on helping participants to become disciple-making leaders, we have made a lot of noise in speeches and in print about two important statements that are both vital to the message of this book:[10]

- You can't make a Christlike disciple from a non-discipleship gospel.
- The gospel you preach determines the disciples you make.

These statements show us that even a very aggressive missional effort over the next fifty years that preaches a gospel to the ends of the earth would leave Jesus still waiting to return if it's the wrong gospel. Jesus said, "The Good News about the Kingdom will be preached throughout the whole world, so that all nations will hear it; and then the end will come" (Matt. 24:14).

False gospels say, in one way or another, "Jesus died for your sins, he rose from the dead and ascended into heaven, and he will return someday to gather his church. Everyone who has agreed with this set of religious facts is a Christian. By the way, you don't need to do anything about it; in fact, you *can't* do anything about it because it is all by grace."

As the late theologian and author Dallas Willard once quipped, "We have not only been saved by grace, we have been paralyzed by it."[11] The church today is truly paralyzed, and it's largely because of a contorted view—even deification—of grace. As a whole, the church lacks commitment to making disciples through its ordinary members on a global scale. Leaders do not expect us to make and multiply disciples, so we're not doing it. As long as we preach the wrong gospel, Jesus' work won't be completed; only a small fraction of lives will be changed.

Non-discipleship gospels may be advanced through various powerful forms of media, but they won't multiply and transform lives of disciples who make still more disciples. These gospels can't do it. The ways and means that Jesus prescribed have not changed. To see reproduction and multiplication, we need people with "discipleship DNA." They must have this DNA, no substitutes. Converts as far as the eye can see will never accomplish what a few committed and multiplying disciples can do when given enough time.

If the church continues down the path it's on, the world will be awash with nominal Christians shaped by a gospel that doesn't reproduce, doesn't transform, and doesn't represent the truth. False gospels will insulate and corrupt nations, and those gospels will fail to accomplish God's will.

When the true gospel is preached to all nations, however, Jesus said the end would come: "All nations will hear it; and then the end will come" (Matt. 24:14). Disciples who make other disciples, who in turn make still more disciples multiplied throughout the earth, will preach this gospel. The Danish philosopher and theologian Søren Kierkegaard has a pertinent observation here: "The main difference between an apostle and a genius is that a genius does not speak with authority but has to rely on skill."[12]

The spread of this gospel will come from ordinary people with the authority of the gospel. These people will accomplish more than what the most innovative and technologically savvy group of genius Christians without gospel authority could ever fathom. As we hold up the gospel that Jesus preached, we have power to penetrate every part of society and every corner of the earth. Let's start today by truly understanding the gospel, then proclaiming it broadly into a world of men and women who desperately need all that God has to offer—including the call to follow Jesus in obedience.

2

WAIT, WHAT IS THE GOSPEL?

"A general fog of confusion swirls around [the gospel] these days. When it comes right down to it, Christians just don't agree on what the gospel is—even Christians who call themselves evangelical."

—GREG GILBERT

A number of years ago, a neighbor invited me (Ben) to a barbecue in his backyard one Sunday afternoon. We had lived next door to each other for a couple of years and we had a lot in common: we were about the same age, shared tools with each other, and had come to know and like each other. His name was John, and he wasn't a Christian. He didn't attend a church and never talked about "religion" unless I brought it up.

As we stood barbecuing in his backyard, I was pleasantly surprised when he said to me, "So Christians are always talking about 'the gospel.'" Then, looking directly at me, he asked, "What *is* the gospel?" For months, I'd been praying that he would be open to talking about Jesus. What an amazing opportunity! The problem was—in this incredible evangelistic moment—my mind completely froze. I bumbled and stumbled and eventually shared the gospel with John. The experience, however, left me startled (and humbled) at my inability to clearly and succinctly communicate the gospel.

What Is the Gospel?

It seems like such a simple question, doesn't it? But if you ask ten Christians, you'll get ten different responses. Some people will respond with one-word answers, others with a long, rambling speech, and still others with a silent, awkward stare. Why? If Christians should be crystal clear about one thing, it should be the gospel, right?

The gospel is supposed to be "of first importance" isn't it (1 Cor. 15:3, ESV)? As Christians, we're meant to be "unashamed of the gospel," aren't we (Rom. 1:16, ESV)? But how can it be "of first importance," and how can you be "unashamed" of it when you're not crystal clear on what it is?

Unfortunately, it's all too common for Christians to erupt and argue at the simple question, "What is the gospel?" A lack of clarity about the gospel has led to a lot of disunity in the church. This lack of clarity rears its ugly head in various forms in local churches and Christian settings. For example, a young, seminary-trained man who used to be on our (Ben's) church staff team was going through the church's ordination process to become a pastor. As part of this process, our elders asked him to preach a sermon and succinctly articulate the gospel. The pre-selected Bible passage was primed for a gospel message, but he didn't do it; in fact, he *couldn't* do it in that moment. Afterward, when we asked him to summarize the gospel in writing, he turned in a ten-page paper! If you don't know what the gospel is, you won't be able to articulate it clearly and succinctly—no matter how smart you think you are.

The problem isn't that Christians aren't talking about the gospel. We are. In fact, it seems like everything in the Christian subculture of America is tagged with *gospel-driven* this and *gospel-centered* that. We talk a lot about the gospel, but if you really listen, that's exactly what it is—it's just talk *about* the gospel.

There's lots of talk about the gospel, in general terms, but precious little about what the gospel actually is! In churches all across America, this gospel talk has left many people thinking, *we know the gospel*, when, in fact, they don't. Something is really wrong when Christians are confused about the true nature of the gospel, or worse still, when they have become numb to it.

The bottom line is this: we can no longer assume people know what the gospel is, even if they say they are Christians or attend church regularly. If you start asking people the simple question "What is the gospel?" unfortunately, you'll quickly find what we've seen.

Increasing Confusion and Different Gospels

The first-century church wasn't confused about the gospel. They were crystal clear about it. As New Testament scholar C.H. Dodd writes: "No Christian of the first century had any doubt what [the gospel] was."[1] Jesus himself taught the gospel to his apostles, who passed it on to the early church. Even Paul—who wasn't one of Jesus' original twelve, but became an apostle later—received the gospel from Jesus himself. Then, Paul took his gospel to the other "pillar" apostles in order to confirm that his gospel was authentic (Gal. 1:11-2:2).

All of Jesus' apostles passed on the gospel to faithful men and women who, in turn, passed it on to others (2 Tim. 2:2). Clearly, the first-century church knew the gospel with precision. They had a clear understanding of it and could communicate it succinctly. They even defined it to the point that they could effectively share it, and they knew when they had passed it on to others (1 Cor. 15:1-2). When the first-century church leaders preached the gospel with this level of clarity, we saw the gospel's power unleashed. Their preaching began to change the world.

Something has changed in the church since then. The gospel that was crystal clear to the first-century church and began a world revolution isn't as clear to the twenty-first century church. Not only is there confusion, but also the church's lack of clarity has led to an escalation of churches that preach a false gospel. This reality should cause us all to sit up, pay attention, and take a good, hard look at the gospel we're preaching. Hebrews 2:1 warns: "We must listen very carefully to the truth we have heard, or we may drift away from it." We need a gospel renaissance.

At various points along the timeline of history, the church has drifted from preaching Jesus' gospel to instead peddling different gospels, which are nothing more than cheap, powerless imitations. In my book, *Conversion and Discipleship*, I (Bill) have identified five different "gospels" being preached today: the forgiveness-only gospel, the gospel of the left, the prosperity gospel, the consumer gospel, and the gospel of the right.[2]

> **Different Gospels**
>
> 1. Forgiveness Only   4. Consumer
> 2. Gospel of Left   5. Gospel of Right
> 3. Prosperity

Each of these gospels sounds different, emphasizes different theological preferences, and calls people to different responses—and none of them includes discipleship. They all separate conversion from discipleship, thus making discipleship optional. This separation should be deeply disturbing to the church. Not only are we cloudy about what the true gospel is, but we're also surrounded with all kinds of different, false gospels, which, as we said earlier, are really no gospels at all (and Paul says this in Galatians 1:7).

A Discipleship Revolution

If we're going to see revival in twenty-first century churches across America, it's not going to happen without a discipleship revolution. This revolution needs to happen everywhere—in Baptist churches in Missouri, in Anglican churches in Arizona, in Pentecostal churches in Pennsylvania, in non-denominational churches in California, and beyond. It will never happen, however, unless and until the church returns to preaching the gospel Jesus preached.

Unlike the various false gospels we listed above, the gospel that Jesus preached didn't separate conversion from discipleship. For Jesus, discipleship wasn't an optional "add-on." His gospel didn't just call people to pray a little prayer for their sins to be forgiven so they'd get to heaven when they died. When you read the four Gospels in the New Testament, do you ever see Jesus call people to respond to his gospel like this? No, Jesus' gospel called people to follow him no matter the cost and without conditions or excuses—to the end. Jesus never taught that you could be a Christian and not be his disciple.

Our First Assumption

As we stated above, this book has two underlying assumptions, which we want to make clear. The first is that you cannot make Christlike disciples from a non-discipleship gospel. We can capture the primary call of Jesus' gospel in two words: "Follow me." Following Jesus involves much more than just praying a one-time prayer for the forgiveness of your sins. It also means that the longer we think people can be Christians without being disciples (that they can believe in Jesus without following him), the more we'll see our best disciple-making efforts fail (no matter how sincere we might be or how much money we might spend).

Non-Discipleship Gospel = Unchristlike Convert

Your church can hire a discipleship pastor, buy the best discipleship curriculum, invite the most dynamic discipleship speakers to your church, and encourage the whole congregation to start making disciples—and it might work for a while. But if you continue preaching a non-discipleship gospel, the early blaze of glory that started with your discipleship efforts will soon burn out. We know this because we've lived it.

The church where I (Ben) have been the senior pastor for the past seven years (Cypress Community Church in Salinas, California) is also my first experience as a senior pastor. When I arrived, I knew we needed to start making disciples, but I had very little idea of how to make that happen despite having a Master's of Theology degree and ten years of ministry experience. So I prayed, read books, and talked with other pastors. I found that I wasn't alone in being a pastor who didn't know how to create a disciple-making movement at my church. I should have waited longer. I didn't. Instead, I went ahead and rolled out a new discipleship initiative for our congregation like I was rolling out a red carpet.

The discipleship initiative at Cypress began with a short six-week, high-energy sermon series on discipleship. It culminated with a discipleship weekend led by a national discipleship expert who came to the church and taught a discipleship seminar on Friday and Saturday with a sermon on Sunday. Our "hired gun" did an excellent job. It was awesome! I was so excited and so were a lot of people in the church.

Our church staff signed up almost one hundred people into discipleship groups. We bought them all the best discipleship curriculum money could buy, gave them a page of detailed instructions on what to do, and set them loose on an incredible disciple-making adventure. Overnight, our church went from zero discipleship groups to more than thirty. It was great!

Within a year, three groups were left. That wasn't great. I was disappointed and disillusioned.

In hindsight, I realized that I expected the right discipleship tools to do the trick. But there was a fatal flaw with my amazing, well-funded discipleship initiative: I hadn't started with the gospel. Because I hadn't begun with a close examination of the gospel I was preaching, we were trying to make Christlike disciples while I was still preaching a non-discipleship gospel.

Our Second Assumption

The second underlying assumption is that *the gospel you preach determines the disciples you make*. If you preach a forgiveness-only gospel, you will make forgiveness-only disciples—people who think they don't need to obey Jesus' commands, can go on sinning, and that God's grace will abound all the more for them (Rom. 6:1).

If you preach a consumer gospel, you'll make consumer disciples—people who "believe" in Jesus only so long as they get something out of it and it doesn't make them too uncomfortable. As soon as consumer disciples feel

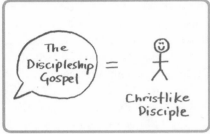

like following Jesus is too hard or inconvenient for them, they tap out. And so on with the various gospels people preach today. But if you preach Jesus' gospel—which we are calling "the discipleship gospel"— then, and only then, do you have the opportunity to make Christlike disciples. When you preach the true gospel, which calls people to be disciples and to make disciples (as Jesus did), you'll witness the multiplication of Christlike disciples.

Understanding these two underlying assumptions should help you realize that when you connect the gospel to discipleship, as Jesus did, it empowers disciple making in your church. Knowing Jesus' gospel of discipleship also helps us see the continuity between belief and obedience. When Jesus called people to believe in the gospel, he assumed that obedience wasn't detached from belief but rather the fruit of it (Mark 1:15).

Now, if you've got alarm bells going off in your head because this sounds like a form of works-salvation, the old lordship-salvation debate, or even an attack on God's grace, let's talk. The discipleship gospel is a call for the church to return to the gospel that Jesus preached, a gospel that has seven essential elements. Without these seven elements, we're proclaiming a false gospel. Let's look at each of these elements.

3

THE ESSENTIAL ELEMENTS OF JESUS' GOSPEL

"My plea is that we go back to the New Testament to discover all over again what Jesus' gospel is."

—SCOT MCKNIGHT

When we speak of the gospel that Jesus preached, it's critical that we examine the New Testament Gospels. Matthew, Mark, Luke, and John are inspired records that reveal Jesus' gospel to us. While you could use any of the four Gospels, we have chosen to primarily use Mark's account for the purposes of this book because biblical scholars generally accept that Mark wrote his Gospel before the others, giving us the first written record of Jesus' life and teachings.[1] Another reason, and more to the point, is that Mark's Gospel clearly reveals Jesus' gospel in two specific passages: Mark 1:14-17 and Mark 8:27-31.

Jesus' own words in these scriptures make it clear that there are seven essential elements of his gospel: four declarative statements, which form what we might say is technically "the gospel proper,"[2] and three imperative responses. Each of the seven elements is not only deeply embedded with discipleship; they also call us to it. In this chapter, we're examining several passages to discover these seven essential elements.

The Word "Gospel" Itself

Before we begin unpacking each of the elements, we need to lay a foundation by addressing several matters which will help us create categories and language that breed clarity. Let's begin with the word "gospel" itself because its meaning is extremely informative in our quest to define Jesus' gospel.

The English word "gospel" finds its origins in the Greek word *euangelion*, which literally means "Good News." In ancient times, *euangelion* was used to describe an announcement of victory or celebration heralded through the streets for all to hear. As such, the ancient idea of *gospel*, or Good News, is a declaration (Psalm 96:2-3). This helps us make sense of why insightful New Testament scholars like Scot McKnight speak of the gospel as being "a narrative declaration" about Jesus.[3] (We'll get into what "narrative declaration" means below when we define the discipleship gospel.) Correctly understood, the gospel is a Scripture-based declaration about Jesus—*who* Jesus is, *what* he has done, *how* he fulfills all Scripture, and *how* he calls us to respond to him.

Declarations and Responses

The gospel, a narrative declaration of Christ's story, has two aspects to it. First, there are four *declarative statements* to the gospel, which are about *who* Jesus is and *what* he has done. In this sense, the gospel truly is all about Jesus. We can call the declarative statements, as we mentioned, "the gospel proper." Distinguished from the responses of Jesus' gospel, this is the first aspect of the gospel. The second aspect of the gospel is Jesus' *imperative statements* that call for our response to the gospel. They are how we should act when we hear the gospel.

Now, while the imperative responses to the gospel are not *the gospel proper* in the purest sense, they are, in fact, essentially attached to it. We can't rightly detach the imperative responses to the gospel from its declarative statements. If people don't respond to the gospel in the way Jesus calls them to, they won't be saved. In other words, while we can *distinguish* between the declarative and imperative responses of the gospel, we must not *separate* them. They are critically connected. Jesus didn't disconnect them, and neither should we. Together they form the seven essential elements of Jesus' gospel. As we discover the seven elements, it's helpful to remember these two categories:

- Declarative statements that make up the gospel proper
- Imperative calls to action that are our responses

The gospel's declaration and our responses to it are like a wedding ceremony. The pastor makes declarative statements about what the couple is doing, and by responding to what he says, they enter into the covenant of marriage. When was the last time you went to a wedding and the bride and groom refused to answer the pastor's questions? Jesus calls us to respond just like a pastor expects the bride and groom to respond at a wedding ceremony. Unless we respond to the Good News, we haven't accepted it.

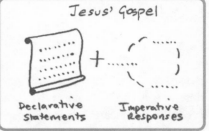

We emphasize this point because there is a trend in the postmodern age to put the Good News before people in a very attractive package without calling upon them to act on it. There seems to be a fear of putting anyone on the spot. This, of course, doesn't work because it's impossible to have a gospel without a call to action.

With these things in mind, let's unpack these two aspects of Jesus' gospel by looking at the four declarative statements of the gospel (the gospel proper) and the three gospel imperatives that go with it.

Four Elements in Mark 1:14-17

In Mark 1:14-17, we see Jesus begin to proclaim the gospel with one declarative statement of the gospel along with the three imperative responses. This brief passage is extremely important for understanding Jesus' gospel because it's rare to find such specificity in the four Gospels. Generally, the Gospel writers tell us *that* Jesus preached, not *what* he actually said. For example, Luke 20:1 says, "Jesus was teaching the people in the temple and preaching the gospel," which tells us *that he preached* but not *what he said* (ESV). In Mark 1:14-17, we're told *what* Jesus actually said when he preached the gospel.

Pay careful attention to his words:

> Now after John was arrested, Jesus came into Galilee, proclaiming the gospel of God, and saying, "The time is fulfilled, and *the kingdom of God is at hand*; *repent* and *believe in the gospel*." Passing alongside the Sea of Galilee, he saw Simon and Andrew the brother of Simon casting a net into the sea, for they were fishermen. And Jesus said to them, "*Follow me*, and I will make you become fishers of men." And immediately they left their nets and followed him. And going on a little farther, he saw James the son of Zebedee and John his brother, who were in their boat mending the nets. And immediately, he called them, and they left their father Zebedee in the boat with the hired servants and followed him.

—MARK 1:14-17, ESV
(emphasis ours)

Before we consider the specific gospel elements this passage reveals, take note that it expressly states that Jesus was "proclaiming the gospel" (v. 14). It couldn't be clearer—this is a gospel passage! People say all kinds of things are part of the gospel by proof texting and taking Bible verses out of context. But using Mark 1:14-17 as an anchor text is different. This passage not only expressly states *that* Jesus was sharing the gospel, but it also specifies *what* he preached as part of the gospel. That's why these verses are vitally important to our understanding of Jesus' gospel. So when Jesus began proclaiming the gospel, what did he say? Let's take a closer look.

Jesus said, "The kingdom of God is at hand" (v. 15). This is the major declarative statement of his gospel in Mark 1:14-17. The three imperatives come immediately after: "Repent," Jesus said, "believe in the gospel," and in verse 17, "follow me." For clarity, we have summarized these essential elements into a concise list of headlines (we'll dig much deeper into each one below):

- God's *kingdom* is here
- *Repent* of sin
- *Believe* the gospel
- *Follow* Jesus

One reason it's important to distinguish between the declarative statements *of the gospel* and the imperative responses *to the gospel* is to help us understand that the imperative responses are actually *part of the gospel*. In fact, we might say that they are so critically connected that *you can't have one without the other*. As such, it's not enough to hear that "the kingdom of God is at hand." Jesus made it crystal clear that this declaration demanded a response! When he called his first disciples to *repent* and *believe* in the gospel (his declaration), he made it crystal clear what their (and our) response should be. These two imperatives are the first steps of *following* Jesus.

We use the word "imperative" to describe these three specific responses not only because they are in the "imperative" mood in Greek and in English grammar, but also (and more importantly) because Jesus makes his calls to action imperative to the gospel—in the sense that they are essential to the gospel. That is, we can hear the declarative statements of the gospel, but if we don't *repent*, *believe* in the gospel, and *follow* Jesus, we won't be saved! It's disruptively simple.

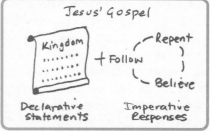

As you consider these four elements revealed in Mark 1:14-17, are you struck by the centrality of God's kingdom and the inclusion of following Jesus as an essential element of the gospel? These two elements are not common in gospel preaching today! While we'll look at these two elements in much greater detail below, it will be helpful to begin to understand how God's kingdom and following Jesus are essential elements of the gospel.

God's Kingdom and Following Jesus

For Jesus' audience, the Good News was that God's kingdom was at hand—it had arrived here on earth! Let this sink in. Jesus repeatedly called his message "the gospel of the kingdom of God" (Luke 4:43). God's kingdom is essential to Jesus' gospel. Simply put, we can't fully grasp Jesus' gospel without knowing about God's kingdom.

At this point, are you asking yourself, *Do I know what the kingdom of God is? Can I clearly communicate what it is to someone else? How many times have I shared the gospel and not mentioned God's kingdom? Can I truly say I've shared Jesus' "gospel of the kingdom of God" if I haven't said anything about God's kingdom?* We'll consider these questions about the kingdom of God more below. For now, note how central and prominent the kingdom of God is to the gospel—it was the very first thing Jesus said about it!

In the same way that the kingdom is vital to Jesus' declaration, his call to *follow* is also an essential element of his gospel. It's one of three *imperative responses* to the gospel that we see in Mark 1:14-17. It's the element that pushes us to realize that Jesus didn't call people to a mere decision of the mind, but to live an entirely new life. Of all the gospel elements, following Jesus might be the most neglected one in our day. We've been led to believe that a one-time prayer for the forgiveness of our sins is enough, that this is all that's required. As soon as you add Jesus' call to follow him to the gospel, it radically changes the gospel. It transforms the gospel into what Jesus originally intended to be "the discipleship gospel."

We're spending some time introducing *God's kingdom* and *following Jesus* now because these are two elements are often absent from "gospel" proclamations today. In fact, they're usually not mentioned at all. To not say a word about God's kingdom and to leave out Jesus' call to follow him from our gospel proclamations renders our "gospel" to be a non-discipleship gospel. And non-discipleship gospels do not lead people to become maturing and multiplying disciples. We'll get into more detail on these things in Part 2, but for now, allow these things to start to germinate in your mind.

Mark 1:14-17 reveals four essential elements of the gospel Jesus preached:

- God's kingdom is here
- Repent of sin
- Believe the gospel
- Follow Jesus

But there are seven elements of Jesus' gospel in total. Let's look at the three others in Mark 8:27-31.

Three Elements in Mark 8:27-31

In the context of Mark's Gospel as a whole, chapter 8 is not only at the middle of his Gospel, but it's also the turning point—theologically, geographically, and also topically with regard to Jesus' revelation of the gospel. Jesus reveals three more elements of his gospel here.

Bible teachers generally accept that there is a two-year gap between Mark 1:14-17 and Mark 8:27-31.[4] For two years, Jesus proclaimed that "God's kingdom was at hand" before he revealed the three other declarative statements of the gospel. These elements in Mark 8 are, in one sense, an extrapolation of *God's kingdom is here*. In other words, the three declarative statements go into more detail about how God's kingdom has come—through Jesus of Nazareth! He is the king of God's kingdom and he is a king who came with a cross rather than a crown.

The epicenter of Mark 8 is the Apostle Peter's confession that Jesus is the Christ. It triggers a lot of change, especially in the focus of Jesus' ministry. Read the text carefully and look for the other three elements of Jesus' gospel:

> And Jesus went on with his disciples to the villages of Caesarea Philippi. And on the way He asked His disciples, "Who do people say that I am?" And they told him, "John the Baptist; and others say, Elijah; and others, one of the prophets." And He asked them, "But who do you say that I am?" Peter answered Him, "You are the Christ." And He strictly charged them to tell no one about Him. And He began to teach them that the Son of Man must suffer many things and be rejected by the elders and the chief priests and the scribes and be killed, and after three days rise again.
>
> —MARK 8:27-31, ESV

These verses represent a major moment of gospel revelation, particularly as it relates to who Jesus is. Jesus reveals the three remaining elements of the gospel here: that he is the *Christ*, that he would *die*, and that he would *rise* from the dead after three days.

It helps to understand the power of Peter's confession in light of all the opinions people had expressed about who they thought Jesus was in the first eight chapters of Mark's Gospel:

- His family thought he was out of his mind (Mark 3:21)
- The scribes thought Jesus was possessed by Satan (3:22)
- The people of Capernaum called him a teacher (5:35)
- The people of Nazareth thought of him as a carpenter (6:3)
- King Herod believed he was John the Baptist resurrected (6:16)
- Some said he was Elijah (8:28)
- Others said he was one of the prophets (8:28)

Surprisingly, while many others had declared their beliefs about Jesus' identity, his disciples hadn't said anything about who they believed him to be—that is until Mark 8. The Twelve asked about Jesus' identity in Mark 4:41 with the question, "Who is this?" Before Mark 8, they had said nothing else about it. Fascinating, isn't it? Everyone else had expressed an opinion about who they thought Jesus was, but not his disciples.

Then in Mark 8:29, when Jesus asked the Twelve, point blank, "Who do you say I am?" Peter's response was powerful—so powerful: "You are the Christ." This is the first time in Mark's Gospel that a human had called Jesus "the Christ." The demons had recognized Jesus as the Christ, but no person had called him "Christ" until Peter in Mark 8:29. When Peter makes this theologically loaded statement with great Old Testament significance, it's a profound moment in Mark's Gospel.

It's as if Peter's confession trips an alarm wire. As soon as one of his disciples confesses him as the Christ, Jesus immediately begins teaching the Twelve about his impending death at the hands of the Jewish religious establishment and his third-day resurrection. In fact, he teaches the Twelve about his death and resurrection three times in three successive chapters (Mark 8:31; 9:31; 10:33-34). This trifecta of predictions begins with Peter's confession, also signaling a massive shift in Jesus' discipleship strategy with the Twelve. From Mark 8:27-31 onward, Jesus spent his time almost exclusively with the Twelve, teaching them the true cost of discipleship (Mark 9:30-31).

Here, we begin to get a sense for how critical a turning point in the narrative and how theologically weighty this passage really is. It also gives us a sense for the essential nature of the statements in Mark 8:27-31 with regard to Jesus being the *Christ*, his *death*, and his *resurrection*. These are the three remaining declarative statements of the gospel—Jesus' gospel.

Now, if you were paying careful attention to Mark 8:27-31, you noticed that the word "gospel" doesn't appear anywhere. Mark 1:14-17 expressly states that Jesus was "proclaiming the gospel," but Mark 8:27-31 does not. It's

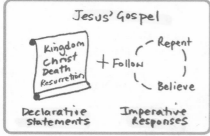

obviously a theologically stout passage, but it doesn't explicitly state that it's a *gospel* passage. This is, in part, because Mark 8:27-31 was *a prophecy* of Jesus' death and resurrection. Jesus hadn't actually died and been resurrected yet. It was only after Jesus' resurrection that the disciples began to understand that his prophecy about these three elements were essential to the gospel. That said, how can we know for certain that the three elements revealed in Mark 8:27-31 are truly essential elements of Jesus' gospel?

While Mark 8:27-31 doesn't specifically state that Jesus being the *Christ*, his *death*, and his *resurrection* are elements of the gospel, Paul makes this clear in 1 Corinthians 15. In fact, it's no overstatement to say that 1 Corinthians 15:1-5 is one of the most important gospel passages in the entire New Testament.

As you'll see, this passage confirms that the three elements revealed in Mark 8:27-31 are, indeed, essential elements of Jesus' gospel.

The Importance of 1 Corinthians 15

Pay careful attention to the inspired words of the Apostle Paul in 1 Corinthians 15:1-5. Look for the three essential elements we noted in Mark 8:27-31:

> Now I would remind you, brothers, of the gospel I preached to you, which you received, in which you stand, and by which you are being saved, if you hold fast to the word I preached to you—unless you believed in vain. For I delivered to you as of first importance what I also received: that *Christ died for our* sins in accordance with the Scriptures, that He was buried, that *He was raised* on the third day in accordance with the Scriptures, and that He appeared to [Peter], then to the twelve.
>
> —1 Corinthians 15:1-5, ESV
> *(emphasis ours)*

Much has been written about the theological and historical significance of this passage (more than we'll unpack here), but we want to underscore just how important it is, especially as it relates to the gospel. Paul's words here are critical for a proper understanding of the gospel, not to mention our understanding of Jesus' resurrection—the linchpin of the gospel.[5]

In the first verse of 1 Corinthians 15, Paul expressly states that he is writing about "the gospel." Like in Mark 1:14-17, this scripture expressly states that it's a gospel passage. Paul reminds the Corinthians of the gospel he had preached to them, which they received, and by which they were being saved. He states, quite emphatically, that the gospel is of "first importance." Clearly, he's talking about the actual message of the gospel.

Stunningly, 1 Corinthians 15:1-5 is almost an exact mirror of Mark 8:27-31 and only an expansion of the essential elements. Both passages speak of Jesus being the Christ. In 1 Corinthians 15, though, we're told that Jesus not

Mark 8	1 Corinthians 15
1. Christ	Christ
2. Killed	Died for our sins
3. Rise again	Raised according to the Scriptures

only died, but that he died for our sins. We also learn that Christ's resurrection wasn't unforeseen, but was foretold long ago, according to the Scriptures. What Jesus predicted would happen in Mark 8—his death and resurrection—did happen. In light of these prophecies being fulfilled, Paul goes into greater depth into their significance in 1 Corinthians 15.

First Corinthians 15 confirms that the three elements revealed in Mark 8 are, in fact, essential declarative statements of the gospel. Paul also adds multiple layers of theological significance to Jesus' death and resurrection. In this way, Paul's words in 1 Corinthians 15:1-5 are critically important in helping us gain clarity on what the gospel is.

Two Gospel-Related Questions

Before we move on, there are two other things worth highlighting in 1 Corinthians 15:1-5. First, we should ask ourselves: if the four elements Jesus revealed in Mark 1:14-17 are so essential to the gospel, why doesn't the Apostle Paul mention any of them anywhere in 1 Corinthians 15:1-5? Paul didn't write anything about God's kingdom, repentance, belief, or following Jesus in 1 Corinthians 15:1-5. Why didn't he? The answer to this question has to do with the fact that 1 Corinthians 15:3-4 is a summary statement.

Paul's summary of the gospel here appears to be a creed-like statement with Paul reducing the gospel to its absolute essence.[6] His original readers, the first-century Christians of Corinth, would have understood this. They would have received 1 Corinthians 15:3-4 as a summary of the gospel, the briefest of summaries, knowing that Paul wasn't excluding God's kingdom, repentance, belief, and following Jesus from the gospel. The language he used signaled to them that these elements were implied based on the creed-like structure of this statement. For example, to state that Jesus is "the Christ" was to recognize him as God's anointed king. As such, Jesus brought the coming of God's kingdom. While this needs to be spelled out for us today, it was implied to the first-century audience because that kind of language was more commonplace.

Likewise, the truth that Jesus is the Christ implicitly demands a response. There's no neutral ground when it comes to receiving the Christ. There's no room to sit on the fence, so to speak. You either receive Jesus of Nazareth as the Christ—by repenting, believing, and following Jesus—or you reject him. The first-century Christians understood this when they read Paul's gospel summary in 1 Corinthians 15:3-4. They knew that Paul wasn't excluding the imperative responses to the gospel; rather, they were implied.

So, if we recognize 1 Corinthians 15:3-4 as a summary statement of the gospel, we must also realize that while Paul mentions only three elements of the gospel directly, all seven are implied.

Another aspect of 1 Corinthians 15:1-5 has to do with the repeated phrase, "in accordance with the Scriptures." This presents the second gospel-related question: what is the significance of this repeated phrase? It's not merely a nice tag-on at the end of these verses or just a mnemonic device to help people memorize this creed-like statement of the gospel. Rather, it invokes the whole Old Testament story and makes Jesus' death and resurrection the climax of the gospel narrative. By using the words "in accordance with the Scriptures," Paul is calling our attention to the fact that Jesus of Nazareth is the beautiful fulfillment of Israel's entire Old Testament story.[7] The phrasing communicates that the whole Bible affirms that Jesus is, indeed, the Christ!

One thing that's helpful to remember is that Paul spent a lot of time defending himself. The crux of his defense was often Jesus' resurrection. It's important to note that the truth of Jesus' resurrection didn't come to us from secular minds, but from divine revelation. When Peter declared that Jesus was the Christ, Jesus said: "Blessed are you, Simon Bar-Jonah! For flesh and blood has not revealed this to you, but my Father who is in heaven" (Matt. 16:19). Paul defends the faith based not on human reason but on the truth of the resurrection. According to Paul, without this revelation, the world is over. It's hopeless, and despair will reign.

We like the story of two men talking on an airplane. After a long debate, one said, "There is one thing I'm sure of—that there is no such thing as absolute truth." The other man, a Christian, responded, "Are you absolutely sure about that?" Paul was sure about Jesus—that Jesus was the Christ, that he died, and that he was resurrected. He wanted us to be sure of these truths, as well.

First Corinthians 15:1-5 has profound significance for the gospel. Most significantly for our current purposes is that it confirms that the three elements Jesus revealed in Mark 8:27-31 are, indeed, essential elements of the gospel he preached.

The Seven Essential Elements

In this chapter, we've discovered the seven elements of the gospel that Jesus preached. There are four declarative statements: God's kingdom is here, Jesus is the Christ, Jesus died for our sins, and Jesus was resurrected on the third day. These four statements form "the gospel proper." There are also three imperative responses that are critically connected to the declarative statements: repent of sin, believe the gospel, and follow Jesus (Mark 1:14-17; Mark 8:27-31; 1 Corinthians 15:1-5). Each of the seven elements find their origin in Jesus himself, and each element comes from a passage expressly stating it's a gospel passage.

Knowing the seven elements of Jesus' gospel is helpful in many ways. For instance, memorizing the seven elements provides a way to evaluate the gospel we share with people who aren't following Jesus. As we share the gospel with others, we can ask ourselves questions to see if we have indeed truly shared the gospel:

- Have I helped them understand that following Jesus means entering into a new realm of life called God's kingdom?
- Do they recognize Jesus as the Christ, God's anointed king?
- Do they believe Jesus died on the cross for their sins and was resurrected from the dead?
- Have I called them to respond to this Good News in the way Jesus did—to repent of their sin, believe the gospel, and follow Jesus?

As such, the seven elements create a helpful checklist that ensures the gospel we believe and share with others is consistent with the gospel Jesus preached.

While it's critical to identify these elements, it's just as important to recognize that the elements are not a complete definition of the gospel. They merely provide the framework for a definition, like a skeleton. So far we've mentioned the seven elements. Now in Part 2, let's dig deeper into their meaning and put meat on the bones of the gospel skeleton, which is formed by the seven elements. Additionally, we'll also see that discipleship is embedded within each of these elements. It will help us glean what the late, great Dallas Willard meant when he wrote "discipleship to Jesus [is] the very heart of the gospel."[8]

PART TWO

THE GOSPEL WE PREACH

Now that we've laid the foundation for a full understanding of the gospel, let's build upon that foundation by considering what Jesus meant by each of the seven elements he revealed. The three passages we considered above—in Mark 1, Mark 8, and 1 Corinthians 15—*mention* the gospel elements, but they don't go into their *meaning*. Now, in Part 2, we'll go deeper into the meaning of each element, observing how each one is critically embedded with discipleship and answering questions you'll encounter when you begin to call people to be disciples and to make disciples as part of responding to the gospel.

As we learned in Part 1, the *four declarative statements* of "the gospel proper" include: God's kingdom is here, Jesus is the Christ, Jesus died for our sins, and Jesus was resurrected on the third day. One way to summarize this Good News is simply saying, "Jesus is king!" We also listed *three imperative responses* that are essential to the gospel—repent of sin, believe the gospel, and follow Jesus. One way to summarize the essence of Jesus' gospel call is to simply say, "Follow Jesus!" As such, declaring that *Jesus is king* and calling people to *follow Jesus* summarizes the gospel of Jesus.

While each element is essential, these first and last ones—*God's kingdom is here* and *follow Jesus*—are worthy of special attention, especially at this juncture in church history because, as we mentioned in Part 1, they are the most neglected elements of gospel preaching today. Consider how rare it is to hear about "the kingdom of God" as part of a gospel message. But if we're going to fully embrace the whole gospel and communicate Jesus' compelling vision for discipleship, we must preach a robust understanding of God's kingdom ruled by Jesus, God's king

Likewise, it's rare to hear Christians in our day relate Jesus' call to follow him with the call of the gospel. Somehow, we've separated the gospel from following Jesus. For instance, while it's common to hear pastors talk about following Jesus, it's rare to hear them call people to follow Jesus as an essential and imperative response to the gospel. As a result, many congregations do not understand that God's amazing grace extends beyond conversion and impacts their daily experience of following Jesus. It's what Dallas Willard meant when he spoke of some Christians being "paralyzed by grace." They don't know how the gospel empowers them as they deny themselves, take up their cross, and follow Jesus.

As we unpack these things in Part 2, we'll begin by gaining a deeper understanding of God's kingdom and how the kingdom is intricately intertwined with Jesus being God's king, his death, and his resurrection. After this, we'll consider in greater depth how Jesus' call to follow him is connected to repentance and faith. If you've been paying close attention, you might object and say, "Hey, that's out of order! It should be repent, believe, and then follow." But they are all connected. Repentance and belief are actually a part of following Jesus, which means we need to first focus on understanding following Jesus before we move on to consider how *repentance from sin* and *believing the gospel* are actually part of the gospel.

4

PREACH THE KINGDOM

"The kingdom of God is where we belong. It is home,
and whether we realize it or not, I think we are all of us
homesick for it."

—FREDERICK BUECHNER

The very first thing Jesus said about the gospel was, "The Kingdom of God is at hand" (Mark 1:15). This was not only the first, but also the last topic he taught. In Acts 1:3, after his resurrection, Jesus spent forty days with his disciples teaching them exclusively about the kingdom of God! The Gospels record that Jesus referenced God's kingdom more than one hundred times during his public ministry. It was his favorite topic. There's just no question that the kingdom of God was central not only to Jesus' ministry, but also to his gospel.

You may be asking: if Jesus spoke of his gospel as "the kingdom gospel," why are we referring to it as "the discipleship gospel"? After all, Jesus didn't call his gospel "the discipleship gospel" even one time. Not once. So why have we? It's because faith in Jesus as the Christ necessitates obedience, and obedience demands discipleship. Consider the links between discipleship and the kingdom:

- Non-discipleship gospels almost always exclude God's kingdom as an *essential* element.
- Discipleship is essential to every element of Jesus' kingdom gospel.
- Believing in Jesus' kingdom gospel leads to a life of discipleship.
- Discipling people until the kingdom gospel is fully formed in them is the key to making disciples of all nations, which is ultimately about the evangelization of the world.

These four factors reveal again why we're calling Jesus' gospel "the discipleship gospel." We hope to recast the gospel's kingdom emphasis in terms of discipleship so that we can clearly see the intricate link between the two!

While God's kingdom punctuated much of Christ's preaching, it has been conspicuously absent from preaching in twenty-first century American churches. Instead of telling the gospel story of God's kingdom coming

through Jesus Christ, we've reduced salvation to hearing a truncated gospel with a short, one-time prayer tacked on the end. The gospel we often hear today goes something like this: *You have sinned, and sin separates you from God. Jesus died on the cross for your sins. If you believe in Jesus, God will forgive your sins and you will go to heaven when you die. Would you like to believe in Jesus? Great, let's pray the sinner's prayer and you'll be saved.* Boom! Done. Gospel presented. But really? Is that it?

This might be *what we've heard* the gospel to be, but that doesn't mean it *is* the gospel. From our preliminary list of Jesus' seven essential elements of the gospel, we can immediately discern that this is an incomplete gospel. For starters, there's no mention of God's kingdom, Christ's resurrection, or repentance. Not only this, but there is not even a hint of following Jesus, which means it's also a non-discipleship gospel. The question becomes, then, is it a distorted gospel like what the Apostle Paul curses in Galatians 1:8? More on this later, but for now, let's go into more detail about God's kingdom and the gospel.

The gospel that Jesus preached was punctuated by God's kingdom. The different "gospels" being preached today are not. A gospel without God's kingdom isn't Jesus' gospel. In other words, we cannot think we're sharing the gospel if we don't say a word about God's kingdom. As we rebuild our understanding of Jesus' gospel, we must start with the foundational concept of God's kingdom.

What happened during the 1974 Lausanne Conference of World Evangelization is instructive for understanding our great need to work God's kingdom back into the gospel we preach. The great Billy Graham and John Stott were at this conference, and Michael Green, the former head of evangelism and apologetics at Wycliffe Hall at Oxford University, was also present. Green stood up before them all and asked, "How much have you heard here about the kingdom of God?"

No one answered, so he answered his own question, "Not much. It's not our language. But it was Jesus' prime concern."[1] More than forty years later, Michael Green's question still calls out for an answer in churches throughout America. Without God's kingdom, we're not preaching the gospel.

The Kingdom of God: A Definition

What is the kingdom of God? In his pivotal work, *The Gospel of the Kingdom*, George Eldon Ladd defines the kingdom of God as "the rule of God."[2] This simple definition is a helpful starting point: *God's kingdom is God's rule*. To build upon Ladd's definition, we've added the idea of restoration. Our definition of the kingdom of God is this: *The kingdom of God is the restoration of God's rule over all things*.

God's kingdom—his rule—is dynamic. Let's look at three time frames of God's rule:

- God ruled over all things in this earthly realm in the beginning, at creation.
- Since the fall, when sin entered the world, God has been restoring his rule over all things in this earthly realm in such a way that his sovereignty has not impinged.
- On the last day, at Christ's second coming, God will, once again, rule over all things and exercise his will on earth as it is in heaven.

Since creation, God's rule has not been static in this earthly realm. His rule has been constant in the heavenly realms for all eternity, but this isn't the case in this earthly realm. It's why Jesus teaches us to pray, "Your kingdom come, your will be done, *on earth as it is in heaven*" (Matt. 6:10, emphasis ours).

Since the fall, God has been putting all things in place so that this fallen, earthly realm might be restored under his absolute sovereign rule. The teaching of the Scriptures becomes clear on this after Jesus' resurrection. Jesus said in Matthew 28:18 that "all authority in heaven and on earth has been given to me." This wasn't only a stunning entrée into his great commission. It also helps us begin to grasp that Jesus has all authority in heaven and on earth—now! As the writer of Hebrews teaches, even though we don't see everything in subjection to Jesus in this fallen world now, not by a long shot, *nothing* in this fallen world is outside his control (Heb. 2:8). Right now, in these last days, Jesus is bringing everything "under his feet" (Eph. 1:22).

"Kingdom" vs. "New Creation"

The restoration of God's rule over all things and the coming of God's kingdom into the world converge in the life of Jesus. Interestingly, there is a noticeable difference between the way Jesus teaches and the way the apostles write about his teachings. Jesus often spoke about God's kingdom "being at hand," "coming," and "advancing." The apostles, on the other hand, wrote about the same things, but with different language. They used phrases like the "restoration of creation," that those who are in Christ are a "new creation," that "the time for restoring all things" had come with Christ, and that "a new heavens and a new earth" would be established (2 Cor. 5:17; Acts 3:21; Rev. 21:1).

Jesus' *kingdom-coming* language and the apostles' *creation-restoration* language may cause some people to think they were referring to two different things, but they weren't. Actually, they were referring to the same thing, just using synonymous language. In other words, when Jesus spoke of God's kingdom advancing, it was the same as the apostles' message. They were both about God restoring his rule over all creation.

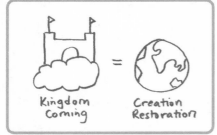

Kingdom Coming = Creation Restoration

This is an important observation for understanding how the kingdom of God relates to the gospel. It helps us grasp that when we proclaim the gospel, speaking specifically about the kingdom of God, we have the biblical freedom to use either Jesus' kingdom-advancing language *or* the apostle's creation-restoration language. Either will do—or even use both! The point is that we must begin to help people grasp that following Jesus means entering into a whole new realm of life, a realm in which God's rule is restored in people's lives through his gospel. In other words, eternal life doesn't begin when we die; it begins when we start following Jesus! God's kingdom has come in the person of Jesus Christ, and as we follow him by faith, we're living in his kingdom.

Recasting the Gospel in Kingdom Language

As we teach ministry leaders about these things through The Bonhoeffer Project (the disciple-making organization that Bill cofounded with Brandon Cook), we have observed how difficult it is for people to recast their understanding of the gospel in terms of God's kingdom. While God's kingdom is essential to Jesus' gospel, they have understood the gospel for so long without it. As we stated earlier, it's a rare thing in our day to hear the gospel preached with God's kingdom included.

As part of our work with The Bonhoeffer Project, we host "cohorts," which are groups of eight to ten ministry leaders who meet for a year to learn to create disciple-making movements in their ministry context. One of the things we do in these cohorts is define the gospel in terms of God's kingdom.[3] It's fascinating to watch people awaken to this as they begin to define the gospel in terms of the kingdom of God. Many know the kingdom of God is important, but they don't understand how it connects to the gospel or, even more to the point, how to communicate the kingdom as an essential element of the gospel. So defining the gospel in this way, at least initially, is challenging for some. We suspect you, too, may find this challenging. I (Ben) remember struggling through this myself in a Bonhoeffer cohort several years ago! It was like strenuously exercising an atrophied muscle—it was hard work.

One of the fascinating aspects of walking with ministry leaders through the process of defining the gospel is seeing how some participants gravitate to Jesus' *kingdom* language while others gravitate to the apostles' *creation* language. Ultimately, it doesn't matter what language you use, only that you use some type of kingdom language. As we communicate the gospel, there's a dire need to help people understand that when they believe in the gospel of Jesus, they are stepping into something far bigger than themselves. They're entering into something God established from the beginning of time, something Christ unleashed with power through his life, death, and resurrection, something God will complete in fullness at the end of time with Christ's second coming, and something that Christ will rule over as king for all eternity—the kingdom of God!

God's Kingdom Is Among Us

As we build up a healthy understanding of God's kingdom, it's critical for us to constantly consider how the kingdom connects to discipleship. One aspect of this connection is the sense in which God's kingdom has come, is coming, and is yet to come. Theologians have dubbed this truth as the "already but not yet" tension of the kingdom of God.[4] Once we get beyond our *how-could-this-be!* reaction to this tension, it's important to identify some of the ways God's kingdom has already come. Our understanding of the kingdom shapes our idea of what it means to follow Jesus.

One specific example of Jesus' teaching that shows us *God's kingdom is here* in the world comes from Luke 17:21 when Jesus declares, "The kingdom of God is in the midst of you." The Greek phrase for "in the midst of you" is notoriously difficult to translate. Some translators prefer to use the translation "within you" and still others use "among you" (both translations work, as far as we're concerned). Whatever your preferred translation, the underlying idea is that the kingdom of God has come into the world through Jesus—*God's kingdom is here.* Don't miss that. Christ inaugurated the kingdom in the world, which means that his kingdom is not only present in the world now, but also that it's actively advancing throughout it!

Wherever Christ Is Ruling

In what ways is God's kingdom already present in the world? And how can it be that his kingdom is already present in the world, but not yet in some places? Here's a helpful way of thinking about the present realities of God's kingdom in the world: *Wherever Christ is ruling, there the kingdom of God is.* Using this as a grid, let's identify various ways that God's kingdom is already present and advancing in the world.

First and foremost, God's kingdom is present in the gospel. The gospel is, as Jesus himself called it, "the gospel of the kingdom" (Luke 4:43). Understood correctly, the gospel is a declaration of Christ's rule, and it's for all people (Luke 2:10). Second, God's kingdom is also present in the lives of all who believe in the gospel and are following Jesus. As Christ rules in our hearts, God's kingdom reigns over our lives (Col. 3:15). Third, when Christ

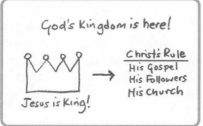

rules in our local churches, God's kingdom is present among us (Rev. 1:6). In other words, when we gather together as a church—fully surrendered to Christ and in total submission to one another—the kingdom of God is among us.

Remember that God's kingdom advances every time a person hears the gospel and begins following Jesus by faith. My friend Bob is a great example of this. I (Ben) have witnessed God's kingdom advance in and through him firsthand. He's a retired salesman, and his wife, Mickey, prayed for fifty years that he would follow Jesus. Two years ago, at seventy-six years old, Bob believed in the gospel and was baptized at our church. God's kingdom invaded his life and marriage, and his life is radically different now.

One year ago, Bob came to me and said, "So, I believe in the gospel, I've been baptized, and I'm attending church every Sunday. Now what?" That's a great question, isn't it? I asked Bob if he'd like to join a discipleship group with me and two other men. We studied the Gospel of Mark together, seeking to put Jesus' teaching into practice one chapter at a time. When Jesus commanded something or we read of him doing something with his disciples in Mark's Gospel, the four of us committed to doing it, too—together (James 1:22). As a new believer, Bob soaked it all up like a sponge.

Through this type of discipleship training, Bob realized that he was being discipled so that he could make disciples. As one disciple maker said, "Only disciples can make disciples." When our discipleship group completed living together through Mark's Gospel, which took us about six months, Bob immediately began his own discipleship group. And his disciple-making labor is bearing fruit, too. Soon after Bob started his first discipleship group, two people from his group were baptized! As I now write this, Bob is leading his second discipleship group and preparing to teach an equipping class for our congregation on making disciples.

Bob is a seventy-eight-year-old man who has been a Christian for two years, and he's making disciples like crazy! God is exponentially multiplying his efforts, and Bob is experiencing the joy of the Lord. He is more than a conversion story and he's more than just a great example of godly retirement; Bob is a clear testimony of how God's kingdom is present and advancing in the world. When people are discipled in the gospel of the kingdom, like Bob was, and when they begin multiplying other disciples, like Bob did, God's kingdom advances rapidly throughout the world! Jesus calls *all* of us, as Christians, to be discipled and to make disciples like Bob.

"Presencing" the Kingdom

Our good friend and the cofounder of The Bonhoeffer Project, Brandon Cook, talks about God "presencing" his kingdom in the world. We like this phrase. It's a clever way of describing God's kingdom as both being *present and advancing* in the world. When Spirit-filled disciples are sent from prayerful churches in the power of the Holy Spirit to love and serve others in the world—especially in ways that lead to people being discipled in the gospel—the "presencing" of God's kingdom multiplies powerfully. This is what Jesus did, it's what he trained his disciples to do, and it's what Jesus commands us to do today—both individually and as members of the church.

My wife, Joni, and I (Ben) experienced this when we planted a church in Cachagua, California, a tiny community made up primarily of two trailer parks. When we arrived in Cachagua, there wasn't any drinkable water in the town. There were water wells, but the fluoride content was too high. Too much fluoride causes your teeth to fall out and your children's bones to break easily—which was happening!

We researched the viability of drilling another well nearby, but the water wasn't any better there. We gave out small bottles of water, but in the long run it was too expensive for our fledgling church to sustain. We organized a dentist to help those whose teeth were adversely affected by the bad water. This dentist, a Christian, served these Cachagua residents free of charge, which was a tremendous blessing. But it still didn't solve the problem.

We kept praying about it and sharing Cachagua's need with others. Then, seemingly out of nowhere, a local Christian businessman who had heard of Cachagua's plight bought both trailer parks as an investment of love and service to the people there. He began making all sorts of improvements, including the delivery of large bottles of pure drinking water to every trailer, every week! The story is a beautiful example of God's kingdom—how God was "presencing" himself and his rule in a tiny, remote community called Cachagua!

As we noted in Part 1, the declaration that "God's kingdom is here" is the first declarative statement of Jesus' gospel. He preached this simple message for two years before he revealed the other three declarative statements of his gospel. God's kingdom wasn't only among the people while Jesus was walking the face of the earth; it's here now—among us. It's "presenced" in the gospel, in the lives of those who are following him by the power of the Holy Spirit, and it's here among those in his surrendered church. Jesus commanded us, as his followers, to seek first the kingdom of God (Matt. 6:33).

The kingdom was the first thing Jesus spoke about when he began preaching the gospel, and it's what he is calling us to seek first even now. May the days be gone when we share the gospel without a word about God's kingdom.

5

PROCLAIM JESUS AS THE CHRIST

"If your life is Christ, then your death will be only more of
Christ, forever. If your life is only Christlessness, then your
death will be only more Christlessness, forever. That's not
fundamentalism, that's the law of non-contradiction."

—PETER KREEFT

Understanding the kingdom helps us understand what it means that
he is the Christ, and it works the other way around, too. Once we
understand what it means that Jesus is the Christ, we see how it's naturally
connected to God's kingdom. In this chapter, we'll discover that declaring
Jesus as "the Christ" is an expression of faith in him as God's anointed king.
In other words, saying "Jesus Christ" is another way of saying that he is the
king of God's kingdom. We shouldn't separate "God's kingdom is here"
from "Jesus is the Christ" because they're inseparable. In the purest sense,
there is no such thing as a kingdom without a king, and it's nonsense to have
a king without a kingdom. It's vital that we discuss not only the kingdom,
but also Jesus as king.

In this chapter, we share more about what it means that Jesus is the Christ
and how surrendering our lives to Christ, which begins by declaring him to
our king, radically impacts our understanding of the discipleship gospel.

Peter's Confession Revisited

When the Apostle Peter confessed that Jesus was "the Christ" in Mark 8:29, it was more than just the turning point of Mark's Gospel; it was the stunning truth! If reading Peter's confession doesn't make you stop and say "Wow!" or "Whoa!" then you may not fully grasp the power of his confession.

"Christ" isn't Jesus' last name. It's a title—a very powerful title with rich Old Testament meaning. To hear someone declare "Jesus is the Christ," which often happens when people are baptized, should cause our mind to stand at attention, our soul to lean in, and our heart to burst with rejoicing and praise for God! To first-century Jews, the word "Christ" was a holy word, reserved exclusively for the long-awaited messiah, God's promised savior for the world. Because we're so far removed from that first-century culture, it's difficult to grasp the full weight of this title or the significance of what Peter says here. To illustrate just how far removed we are from understanding the holiness of the word "Christ," consider the fact that it's often used as a cuss word today.

We begin to grasp the weight of Peter's confession when we observe the critical changes that occur in Jesus' ministry after it. For example, immediately after Peter's confession, Jesus began teaching the Twelve about his death and resurrection, a topic he had never before broached. Also, soon after, Jesus "set his face to go to Jerusalem" (Luke 9:51). It would seem Jesus had been waiting for his disciples to grasp that he was the Christ before shifting his whole focus to the cross. In this sense, Peter's confession seemingly triggered the beginning of the end for Jesus.

In Part 1, we briefly considered the significance of the Apostle Peter's confession. We also took note that the Apostle Paul confirms *Jesus is the Christ*, which we considered as an essential element of the gospel (1 Cor. 15:3). It isn't enough, however, to know factually that Jesus is the Christ or to just utter those words; we need to know what those words mean and believe them with our whole heart. If Jesus isn't the Christ, there is no gospel. If he is—and he is indeed—it means that he is God in the flesh, the anointed king of God's kingdom. What comes to our minds when we think about Jesus being the Christ is essential to our faith in the gospel.

The Meaning of "The Christ"

At the very beginning of Mark's Gospel, he immediately, even abruptly, states that Jesus is the Christ: "The beginning of the gospel of Jesus Christ, the Son of God" (Mark 1:1). Mark also begins downloading, as it were, the meaning of that statement by adding the explanatory phrase, "the Son of God." This helps form our thinking about what it means that Jesus is the Christ. To declare Jesus as the Christ is to believe he is the Son of God, God's one and only Son.[1]

The title "Christ" invokes the weight of the entire Old Testament, indeed all Scripture. In fact, it's one word that encapsulates all of the Bible's teachings about God's promised savior and everything that the Bible reveals about Jesus. Knowing this gives us insight into two truths. First, when we trace the meaning of the word "Christ" back to its origins, it takes us back to the Old Testament Hebrew word for "Messiah." "Christ" comes from the Greek New Testament word that translates the Hebraic Old Testament word for "Messiah." Both terms literally mean "the anointed one." A king was understood to be the anointed one in ancient times. As such, to confess Jesus as "Christ" was to declare that he was God's anointed one, the king of God's kingdom. "Christ," then, means *God's anointed king*.

The second insight we receive from digging back into the Old Testament roots is from Mark 1:2-3, which reveals more of what Mark 1:1 means when Mark's words declare Jesus to be the Christ. The next two verses repeat the words of two Old Testament prophets (Mal. 3:1; Isa. 40:3). Mark, the writer of this Gospel, is showing us, as his readers, that Jesus fulfills these Old Testament prophecies about the Christ. This truth is a game changer. It immediately awakens us to the reality that with the coming of Jesus, Old Testament prophecies and promises about the Christ had begun to be fulfilled by him. His fulfillment of these two prophecies in Mark 1:2-3 indicates that Jesus fulfills other prophecies about the Christ—indeed, all of them.

There are hundreds of prophecies and allusions to the Christ in the Old Testament. As they were inspired to write the New Testament, the apostles went to great pains to point out that Jesus of Nazareth fulfills all Old Testament prophecies about the Christ. For example, in Luke 24:44-49, Jesus explained his resurrection to his disciples by referencing how everything written in the Old Testament—"the Law of Moses and the prophets and the Psalms"—showed that "the Christ should suffer and on the third day rise from the dead." To proclaim Jesus as the Christ, then, is to also understand that Jesus is *the one about whom all Scripture is written* and *the one who fulfills all Scripture.*

Obeying Jesus as King

Now that we have an understanding of what the "Christ" title means, we must also consider the impact of declaring Jesus to be the Christ, which the gospel demands. It's not enough to just say the words; we must declare that Jesus is the Christ in a way that leads to salvation. We do this by proclaiming it with our whole heart and fully surrendering our lives to Jesus. Practically speaking, we should give a newly converted disciple of Jesus the opportunity to publicly declare this immediately before they are baptized. If we truly believe that Jesus is the Christ, it has massive implications on our lives. For starters, it means that we surrender our lives to him as our king, seeking to obey all of his commands (Matt. 28:20).

Matthew Bates, who wrote the provocatively titled book *Salvation By Allegiance Alone*, writes: "The gospel climaxes with the enthronement of Jesus as the cosmic king, the Lord of heaven and earth, even though all too often this portion of the gospel is entirely omitted when it is proclaimed to-day."[2] He makes the case that to declare Jesus to be the Christ is to swear allegiance to him as God's anointed king. "*Faith* in Jesus," he says, "is best described as *allegiance* to him as king."[3] Practically speaking, this means that to declare Jesus to be the Christ is to devote yourself to him in love, serving his purposes and obeying him as king. "This enacted obedience is essential to salvation," Bates states.[4]

When we declare, "Jesus is the Christ," we devote ourselves to him in obedience. Jesus asked a penetrating question about this when he said, "Why do you call me 'Lord, Lord,' and not do what I tell you?" (Luke 6:46). By asking this question, Jesus makes the strong point that if we call him Lord, we should do what he tells us to do; in other words, we should obey him. The Apostle James asked a similar, thought-provoking question: "What good is it, my brothers, if someone says he has faith but does not have works? Can such faith save him?" (James 2:14). The implied answer to this inspired question is, "No, faith without obedience isn't saving faith." Obedience is critical for salvation, which means that it's essential to the gospel.

We see this also in Romans 1:1-6, another critical passage in the New Testament that expressly reveals the content of the gospel. In it, the Apostle Paul directly connects obedience to Jesus with the message of the gospel:

> Paul, a servant of Christ Jesus, called to be an apostle, set apart for *the gospel of God*, which he promised beforehand through his prophets in the holy Scriptures, concerning his Son, who was descended from

David according to the flesh and was declared to be the Son of God in power according to the Spirit of holiness by his resurrection from the dead, Jesus Christ our Lord, through whom we have received grace and apostleship to bring about *the obedience of faith* for the sake of his name among all the nations, including you who are called to belong to Jesus Christ.

—ROMANS 1:1-6

It's not surprising that in this passage, Paul places a heavy emphasis on the truth that Jesus is the Christ. Specifically, he refers to Jesus as either "Christ Jesus" or "Jesus Christ" three times in these six verses. And take note, it also emphasizes that obedience is essential to having faith in the gospel. Specifically, in Romans 1:5, the Apostle Paul writes that the grace we have received in the gospel is "to bring about *the obedience of faith* for the sake of his name among all the nations." This is a purpose statement. In other words, God's purpose for the gospel is bringing about in us obedience to Jesus, who is the Christ.

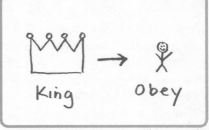

The obedience of the gospel, as we will learn later, is only and ever empowered by the Holy Spirit. In light of these passages of Scripture, then, to say that a person doesn't need to obey Jesus to believe in him, as some people in our day say, is nothing short of a gross misunderstanding of what the Bible teaches about the gospel and about salvation. If you declare Jesus to be the Christ, you are issuing a call to obey him as king.

Recognition by Demons

As we continue to unpack Peter's powerful confession of Jesus as the Christ, it's fascinating to note that the demons recognized Jesus was the Christ without delay—immediately, in fact. This recognition plays an important role in the development of Mark's Gospel. The difference between Peter's confession and the demons' recognition is vital to understand. The demons knew precisely who Jesus was and they said as much two solid years before Peter did. Yet, unlike Peter, they refused to surrender themselves to him as king and submit themselves to his rule.

The Gospel of Luke offers an example of the rebellious recognition of the demons that Jesus was the Christ: "Demons came out of many, crying, 'You are the Son of God!' But [Jesus] rebuked them and would not allow them to speak, because they knew that He was the Christ" (Luke 4:41). But the demons' recognition was a mere external acknowledgement of a fact.

An acknowledgement of the fact that Jesus is the Christ is much different than *the confession* that Jesus is the Christ, which is born out of saving faith. The life-or-death difference here is the difference between heaven and hell. This distinction becomes most evident in the kind of disciples we are and the kind of disciples we make. The Pharisees made disciples, but they made them twice as much children of hell as the Pharisees were (Matt. 23:15).

The distinction between Peter's confession and the demons' recognition suggests that we can know Jesus is the Christ intellectually but not believe him personally. The demons had knowledge, but they weren't willing to surrender themselves to him as king. We can do the same thing. We can know that Jesus is the Christ in our heads, but it's different to lean on Jesus as the Christ in our hearts. When a person expresses faith in Jesus as king, like Peter did, it not only changes the way they view Jesus, but also it enables them to surrender their life to him. Plus, it empowers them to be disciples who deny themselves, take up their cross, and follow him.

As we consider the significance of Jesus being the Christ for our preaching of the gospel, it's critical to understand that confessing Jesus to be the Christ isn't about knowing the right Sunday-school answer or uttering the magic words at our baptism. It is not a matter of head knowledge, but a matter of the heart. If our heart is unwilling to surrender to Jesus as king, it renders whatever words we may say about him as "the Christ" meaningless.

We must realize that it can take time, sometimes a lot of time, for truths like *Jesus is the Christ* to move from our head to our heart or for our knowledge *about Jesus* to be our experience *of Jesus*. It took Jesus' disciples two years before they began to grasp it. As we feel the tension of being in this in-between place—between head and heart—it opens us up to see the transforming impact that discipleship can have on a person's life.

Learning Jesus Is the Christ Through Discipleship

The best way for us to come to know Jesus as the Christ is through discipleship. We say discipleship is "the best way" because it's the way that Jesus modeled for his disciples. The disciples didn't just start confessing Jesus as the Christ; it took some time! What brought Jesus' disciples to the point of confessing him to be the Christ from the heart? Simply stated, it was discipleship. At its core, discipleship is being with Jesus—as we spend time *with him*, our knowledge *about him* becomes our experience *of him*.

Let me (Ben) tell you a story of how one young lady named Amy learned that Jesus is the Christ through discipleship. She visited our church, and since she was a reporter for the local newspaper at the time, when she asked to talk to me after the service, I assumed she was writing a story. Within five minutes of our conversation, though, it was apparent to me that Amy wasn't asking questions for a story; she wanted to know more about Jesus just for herself. She asked great questions, as good reporters do, but about fifteen minutes into our conversation, I asked her a question: "Amy, who do you think Jesus is?" She got quiet and answered, "I'm not sure."

As we began talking about who Jesus was and is, I shared with Amy the helpful grid that C.S. Lewis used in his brilliant book, *Mere Christianity*, to answer this question. Lewis showed that Jesus unequivocally claimed to be the Christ, God's one and only son, and that there are only three logical conclusions to the question. Either Jesus was a *liar, lunatic*, or the *Lord*. Amy didn't have a Bible, so I gave her one and encouraged her to read all the way through one of the Gospels. I told her that as she read it, she should ask herself whether she thought Jesus was a liar, lunatic, or the Lord. Amy left grateful and interested.

I got an email from Amy just a few days later. She was out of town on assignment, but wanted me to know that she had read all the way through Matthew's Gospel. She had several more good questions via email, once again, as all good reporters do. Then, she wrote a simple, short statement like this: "After reading Matthew's Gospel, I don't think Jesus was a liar or a lunatic." I kept reading to see if she expressed faith in Jesus as Lord, but when I got to the end of the email, it wasn't there.

I began seeing Amy at our Sunday service regularly, and she interacted with my wife and me more and more. After several months, we saw Amy, and she said with a big smile: "I don't think Jesus was a liar or a lunatic. I believe that he is the Lord, and I'd like to get baptized." Just like with Jesus' disciples, Amy came to believe that Jesus was and is the Christ through intentional discipleship over a period of time. Looking back over the story—as my wife, Joni, and I journeyed with Amy over a number of months through conversations, emails, answering questions, worshipping together, and increasingly sharing life with one another—Amy went from knowing that Jesus *is the Christ* to experiencing him in her life *as the Christ*. She went from knowing the right answer to believing in Jesus with all her heart, willing to surrender her life to him. Being in an intentional, discipling relationship is the best way to come to know and truly believe that Jesus is the Christ.

Discipleship to Jesus is Being with Christ

This all reveals that there is a connection between being *with Jesus* and coming to the point of *confessing Jesus* as the Christ. Jesus chose the Twelve so they could be *with him*. It was his primary purpose in setting them apart to be his disciples. Mark 3:14-15 says that "[Jesus] appointed twelve (whom he also named apostles) *so that they might be with him* and he might send them out to preach and have authority to cast out demons" (emphasis ours).

Before this passage says Jesus set his disciples apart to preach and cast out demons, it first says that Jesus appointed them *to be with him*. This was Jesus' first and primary purpose in choosing the twelve apostles. For Jesus, discipleship wasn't about getting through a curriculum, as we often do, or training people to "do stuff" for him. Discipleship for Jesus was first and foremost about being with his disciples—being with them so he could influence them to be more like him.

The ultimate goal of discipleship is Christlikeness, and this transformation occurs as we begin living our lives with Jesus and living for his purposes. The fact that Peter's confession of Jesus as the Christ didn't occur until the disciples had spent a lot of time together—two years—shouldn't get lost in all the action (and there is a lot of it in Mark's Gospel).

The Holy Spirit used the disciples' time *with Jesus* to open their hearts *to him*, and while we are not Jesus, as disciple makers in the body of Christ, we make a similar impact by spending time with those we are discipling. After being with him for some time, they not only knew that he was the Christ, but they had experienced him as the Christ. They not only believed in the grace of Christ, but they had also experienced his grace. They not only learned about the forgiveness of the Christ, but they had also heard Jesus say to them personally, "Your sins are forgiven." They had not only heard about the love of the Christ, but their hearts were also burning with love for him (Luke 24:32). It was their being *with him* that caused the truth that he was the Christ to move from their heads to their hearts. The same change happens with us. That's what happened with Amy. This transformation happens best in the context of intentional and loving, discipling relationships.

Now let's drive this point all the way home. In our experience, discipleship groups of three or four are a great way to help people spend time *with Jesus*. As you gather in his name together, study his teaching, pray to him, seek to hear his voice, and put his teaching into practice, you are spending time with him, and more importantly, he is with you. Jesus' presence is a major promise of his great commission. He said, "And behold, *I am with you always*, to the end of the age" (Matt. 28:20, emphasis ours). As we obey Jesus' command to be disciples who make disciples, he is with us *and we are with him*. We'll go into more depth about the transformative environment of discipleship groups later, but for now, remember this: discipleship is one of the greatest ways for knowledge about Jesus as the Christ to become love from the heart for Jesus.

As this chapter shows, the truth that Jesus is the Christ is an essential element of the gospel, and we are convinced that experiencing Jesus through discipleship is the best way for people to come to truly believe this truth and confess it out loud from their hearts. Discipleship, which is intentionally learning to live and love others like Jesus with other Christ followers, not only gives us the opportunity to learn that Jesus is the Christ, but it also gives us the opportunity to experience his presence and his power as the Christ. As we begin to experience Christ's presence, he enables us to live a new life defined by dying to ourselves daily. As we continue to dig into the depths of the essential elements of Jesus' gospel, we begin to see the impact of Christ's death upon our lives.

6

DISCIPLE UNTO DEATH AND RESURRECTION

"To be a follower of the Crucified means, sooner or later,
a personal encounter with the cross. And the cross always
entails loss. The great symbol of Christianity means
sacrifice and no one who calls himself a Christian can
evade this stark fact."

—ELISABETH ELLIOT

The death and resurrection of Jesus of Nazareth are two of the most discussed and debated events in history. The evidence for Jesus' death is overwhelming and, according to historian and New Testament scholar Gary Habermas, there is more historical evidence for the resurrection of Jesus than for any other event in ancient history.[1] In this chapter, we're going to argue that personal faith in Christ's death and resurrection, biblically understood, leads us to die to sin daily and live in the power of Christ's resurrection. While establishing the facts of history has its place, we want to go beyond a mere acknowledgement of the facts here to boil it all down to this biblical truth: if you don't embrace the lifestyle that comes from Jesus' death and resurrection, then your belief in them is faulty. Let's focus on Christ's death first.

If we have faith in Christ's death, then the New Testament beckons us beyond mere intellectual acknowledgement of the cross of Christ. There is a sense in which Christ is calling us to have a faith in a death beyond his own

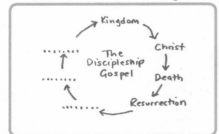

death! If we truly believe in Christ's death, then our faith will lead us to deny ourselves and to take up our own cross, just as Jesus calls all his followers to do in Mark 8:34. It's a call to die to sin in our lives daily. In other words, our faith in Christ's death is supposed to extend to us who also die to sin daily. A common characteristic of many non-discipleship gospels is that they ask people to have faith in Christ's death, but they stop short of calling them to die to sin each day. This marker starts to cut to the core of what the discipleship gospel is all about, and it's exactly what we're going to turn our attention to now.

A Death Beyond Jesus' Death

To the first-century Jew living in Israel, the cross meant one thing—Roman crucifixion. Crosses evoked images of hundreds of Jews, even thousands, crying in agony as they hung from crosses on the hills surrounding Jerusalem. The Romans devised crucifixion to be the absolute worst and most public way to die.[2] The cross was the ultimate symbol of death and oppression. It was also a constant visible reminder for Jews that God was not ruling in Israel—Rome was! As soon as Jesus said following him involved the word "cross," the crowd following him would've stopped dead in their tracks. The cross meant death.

What did Jesus mean by "take up our cross"? First, we need to know that *taking up your cross* is something all followers of Jesus are to do *daily*. While this isn't clear in Mark 8:34, it is clear in the parallel account of Luke 9:23. Second, taking up your cross begins with denying yourself; denying the selfish and sinful desires of your flesh. But it doesn't stop with just denial. Third, it also involves putting those selfish and sinful desires to *death*. We need to *crucify* our sinful desires, to use the cross-language of Jesus. Taking up our cross means putting to death the sinful desires of our flesh every day.

We mustn't sell our interpretation short, though. Taking up your cross for Christ's sake might actually lead to your physical death. Living this kind of "take up your cross" life led to Jesus' death. It also led to all of his apostles' deaths, according to tradition. Why would it be different now? As you think about that, consider this fact: more Christians have been martyred in the last one hundred years than in any century since Christ's crucifixion.[3]

In Galatians 2:20, Paul wrote: "I have been *crucified* with Christ. It is no longer I who live, but Christ who lives in me" (emphasis ours). Repeatedly in the New Testament, we're called to "count ourselves *dead* to sin" and to "put to *death* the deeds of the flesh," and so on.[4] Galatians 5:24 says, "Those who belong to Christ Jesus have *crucified* the flesh with its passions and desires" (emphasis ours). All of this language, and all of these commands find their origin in Jesus' words about *taking up our cross* daily.

People who are truly following Jesus have a faith in Christ's death that leads them to crucify their flesh with its passions and sins. Their belief in Christ's death impacts their daily life because they're learning to deny themselves and take up their cross daily. This is called following Jesus. For someone to say that they believe in Christ's death and resurrection, but then reject their need to put to death the deeds of the flesh is, at the

very least, to have a faith that is badly stunted, if not a faith that doesn't save.

The Gospel Is Not About You!

Three short words transform Jesus' death from a human tragedy of epic proportions into *The Day the Revolution Began*, as N.T. Wright calls his 2016 book by the same name. Those three words are "for our sins."[5] Jesus died *for our sins*. When we truly come to grips with this, it's nothing less than a full-blown encounter with the amazing grace of God Almighty! Many of the non-discipleship gospels that get preached today, however, make the gospel primarily about *me*. People who preach these *me-centered* "gospels" effectively rush through "the Jesus part" and focus on the "what's in for *me*" part. *I* get forgiveness for *my* sin; *I* get to go to heaven when *I* die—it's all about *me*. But the discipleship gospel isn't about *me*; it's about *Jesus*! It's also about others, in the sense that if we truly follow Jesus, we will love others like

Jesus loves us (John 13:34-35). False gospels are *self-centered*; the true gospel is *others-focused*.

As we identify these me-centered gospels, we're not saying that the gospel doesn't have massive implications for us. It does for sure—nothing less than the eternal salvation of our souls. We are simply seeking to resurrect the understanding that Christ's gospel isn't just about us as individuals; it's about something grand and something with great, cosmic, and eternal implications that the *me-centered* gospel doesn't even scratch. That grand and great thing is this: God is reconciling all things to Christ and establishing his eternal kingdom (Col. 1:20)!

Jesus Died for More Than Just Our Sins

Christ's death secured our salvation to be sure, but it also paved the way for the redemption of the whole world. 1 John 2:2 teaches us that Christ's atoning sacrifice was "not for our sins only but also for the sins of the whole world," and Romans 8:22 tells us that "the whole creation" is groaning for the day of its redemption. Christ's death is the catalyst for the restoration of God's rule over all things in heaven and on earth, especially for those people who follow him.

This is the point at which we see God's kingdom colliding with Christ's death. Christ's death broke open the floodgates of God's kingdom-advancing work in the world. Through Christ's death on the cross, God unleashed the power of the gospel to save, he sent the indwelling Holy Spirit to empower believers unto obedience, and Christ began building his church. Not only this, but Christ's death also defeated Satan, conquered death, and smashed sin.[6] This gives us a sense of what it means that the gospel is much bigger than *me*!

In this much broader context, we can understand the gospel's declaration that *Christ died for our sins*. God is establishing an eternal kingdom in which his one and only son, Jesus Christ, is the focal point of all worship (Rev. 7:9-12). Our salvation is ultimately about him!

Christ's Death and Our Sin

Identifying and embracing all of the implications of Christ's death on the cross helps us understand that the gospel isn't all about us. While that's true,

Christ did die *for our sins*. Of all the elements of the gospel, this incredible truth is often the one that penetrates a person's heart, opens them up to God's love, and makes them willing to acknowledge their sin. This truth makes the gospel shockingly personal.

In his letter to the Romans, the Apostle Paul states, "But God shows his love for us in that while we were still sinners, Christ died for us" (Rom. 5:8). This thought-provoking verse confronts us with the incredible, expansive, and deep love of God and also calls our attention to our sin for which he died. Everyone has an internal sense of his or her own sin. Even hardhearted people who won't admit they have sinned still know in themselves that they have sinned. The Bible calls this internal sense of sin our "conscience" (Rom. 2:15). What we know by our conscience, the Bible also clearly states: "We all have sinned and fallen short of the glory of God" (Rom. 3:23).

Encountering God's Love in the Gospel

When the guys that I (Ben) grew up with in Australia later found out I was a Christian, they laughed. When they learned I'd become a pastor, they fell to the ground in hysterics. Of course, I wasn't the church-going type growing up. When people tried sharing the gospel with me—and a few of them did—I ignored them. If they had persisted (which no one ever did) and told me that I was a sinner to my face, there's a good chance I might have punched them in their face. I didn't want anything to do with God, and I definitely didn't want anyone pointing out my sin. I was one lost soul—that is until I was a caddie for my friend, Dean, on the PGA tour and discovered that Jesus had died for my sins. Let me tell you the story.

Dean had been my best friend growing up in Australia. He earned a college scholarship to play golf in the United States and in his final year of college qualified to play golf on the PGA golf tour. He also became a Christian so that when he came back to Australia the Christmas before his rookie season on tour, it was obvious: his life had changed a lot—for the better! At the time, though, I couldn't put my finger on what had changed about him, but there was a new sense of purpose and a peace that wasn't in his life before.

During the holidays, Dean asked me if I would go to the United States to be his caddie on the PGA Tour. It was a no brainer. "Yes!" I said without a second thought. So we spent a year in the United States on the golf tour together. The noticeable change in my good friend's life began to open me up to the gospel.

During our first week on tour, Dean invited me to a Bible study led by Fellowship of Christian Athletes. A number of the professional golfers and their wives attended the study. I had never heard of people studying the Bible, but trusting Dean and being intrigued by the change in his life, I went anyway. I kept everyone at arm's length for two months, but I listened carefully. As I looked on, I was impressed by their faithfulness to go to the Bible study every week. I was even more impressed by their lives outside of the Bible study.

Then on Easter Sunday, Dean took me to church, and the pastor preached the gospel. When the preacher told me I was a sinner, I found my-

self agreeing with him. That was a first! I had always known deep down that I was a sinner, but I'd never been willing to acknowledge it until that day. Then, when the pastor told me of Christ's love—that Jesus died on the cross *for my sins* and that he would forgive my sins—I was over-

whelmed. Jesus overwhelmed me. I had never heard of such love, and the truth that Christ died so that my sins might be forgiven was stunning to me.

The pastor had preached the full gospel that Easter Sunday. While I wasn't aware of it at the time, I listened to a recording of that sermon later, and he had preached all seven elements of the gospel! When he called people to repent, believe, and begin following Jesus, I did just that. My conversion was a Romans 5:5 experience, where God poured his love into my heart by the Holy Spirit. For someone who wanted nothing to do with God just a short time before, it was a radical turnaround. I began following Jesus by faith that Easter Sunday, and I still haven't quite recovered. I hope, by the grace of God, I never do.

I share my story with you here to give you an example of the amazing power of preaching Christ's death without reservation. Do for others what was done for me: preach Christ's death—all the implications of it. Tell of his love and don't leave out sin. Help people understand that the call to believe in Christ's death is a call to live a new life of denying themselves and taking up their own cross daily. When you say this, you communicate that the ongoing reality of our faith in Christ's death is dying to sin each day of our lives. This death to sin frees us from our sin to live a new life in Christ's resurrection power, to which we now turn our attention.

Say More About Resurrection

You cannot be a true follower of Jesus and be saved if you don't believe in Jesus' resurrection. Alternatively, the Apostle Paul states that if Christ was not raised from the dead, our faith is futile and we are still dead in our sins (1 Cor. 15:17). Moreover, if Jesus wasn't raised from the dead, he isn't the Christ and Christianity crashes. There should be no doubt about it: belief in Christ's resurrection is essential to the gospel and for salvation, which is what Jesus and the apostles taught (Matt. 12:38-45; 1 Cor. 15:12-19). No resurrection, no gospel.

While it's rare for someone to argue that belief in Christ's resurrection *isn't* essential to the gospel, Christians commonly emphasize Christ's death over his resurrection when they share the gospel. This approach mistakenly gives hearers the impression that Christ's death is more important than other elements of the gospel, including his resurrection. It sometimes happens when we talk so much about Christ's death that we leave little time, if any, to talk about the importance of his third-day resurrection. We need to preach Jesus' resurrection. It lies at the heart of the gospel message, without which there is no gospel. So, preach it!

A number of years ago, I (Ben) was asked by the principal of a new Christian school in our area to review the school's proposed doctrinal statement. I was impressed that it included a specific paragraph that articulated the gospel. They did a great job of explaining the substitutionary nature of Christ's atonement. When I finished reading the paragraph, however, I realized there wasn't a word about the resurrection—not one word. I shared this with the principal, and his reaction was "Whoops!"

Whoops, indeed.

This mistake is symptomatic of a deep gospel problem in our culture—we emphasize the death of Jesus over his resurrection to the point that we risk preaching a false gospel. It's easy for us to fall prey to this kind of thing if we're not crystal clear on what the gospel is. Let's be clear: without Christ's resurrection, his death is rendered utterly powerless.

Living in the Power of Christ's Resurrection

Faith in Christ's resurrection results in a life of experiencing the power of the resurrection. As the Ephesian Christians followed Jesus, the Apostle Paul prayed that they would experience the power of Christ's resurrection.

Specifically, he prayed they would know "*the immeasurable greatness of his power* toward us who believe, according to the working of his great might that he worked in Christ when he *raised him from the dead*" (Eph. 1:19-20, emphasis ours). That's a powerful prayer, one we should pray for each other today.

Living in the power of Christ's resurrection sounds amazing, but it's also a bit vague and hard to get our heads around. That is until we connect it to the Holy Spirit. Romans 8:11 states, "If the Spirit of him who raised Jesus

from the dead dwells in you, he who raised Christ Jesus from the dead will also give life to your mortal bodies through his Spirit who dwells in you." This verse links Christ's resurrection power with the indwelling Holy Spirit. To live in Christ's resurrection power, then, is to follow Jesus by the Holy Spirit. Specifically, it's to be empowered by the Holy Spirit, who raised Christ from the dead, to *die to sin* and *live in obedience* to Christ. In this way, following Jesus is a daily experience of the gospel. So, how can following Jesus *not* be an essential element of the gospel when following Jesus is a daily experience of the gospel?

Empowered for Obedience

Our point here is this: Christ calls us to follow him, and our faith in his resurrection fills us with power from the Holy Spirit to obey. In other words, Christ has a purpose in filling his followers with resurrection power—obedience. This is the "obedience of faith" that Paul writes about as he lays out the gospel in Romans 1:1-6. Unfortunately, some Christians have the resurrection power of Christ available to them, but they have a stunted faith in Jesus' resurrection, leaving them unaware of the power at their disposal. It's like they're an electrical appliance but their cord is unplugged.

A lot of weird theology is floating around today about obedience. For example, some think that calling for simple obedience is tantamount to teaching works-salvation. Then, others think you can pick and choose the commands of Jesus that you like to obey and you only have to obey them when it's convenient for you. Of course, they wouldn't say this, but they live like it's true. Still others focus so much on their sin that they think their self-absorbed obsession with sin *is* obedience. Whatever the case, bad theology and sometimes even out-right heresy abounds with beliefs about obedience. But the Bible clearly teaches that if you don't obey Jesus, you're not following him.

Jesus was crystal clear about obedience, and his Great Commission is a prime example. He calls his followers to make disciples who "observe all that I have commanded you." The word for "observe" here is synonymous with the word for "obey." Jesus instructed us to obey *all his commands.* "All" means all—no matter how you slice it or dice it. In this way, Christ, who is the resurrected king of God's kingdom, calls for complete obedience from his followers. On more than one occasion, I (Bill) have taught that *you give up the right to say "no" to Jesus when you begin following him.* If you don't do what he says, don't trick yourself into thinking you're following Jesus.

In the midst of all this talk of total obedience, remember that Jesus commands only what he empowers. If he asks us to do something, he'll provide the way for us to do it. That's why, at conversion, God gives us the gift of the Holy Spirit who comes to dwell in us, "to give life to your mortal bodies" (Rom. 8:11). When does this infusion of power occur? Dallas Willard's words are insightful here: "The Holy Spirit meets us in obedience."[7]

This doesn't mean that disciples always choose obedience. You only have to read the New Testament to see that the apostles themselves followed Christ imperfectly. As the Apostle John writes, "If we say we have no sin, we deceive ourselves, and the truth is not in us" (1 John 1:8). Our point here is that following Jesus is defined by obedience, and if we have full faith in Christ's resurrection, then we will believe that his resurrection power enables us to obey him daily. This is what "living in the power of Christ's resurrection" means.

At this point in these pages, we're making a transition from the declarative aspects of the gospel to the imperative aspects of the gospel. We've unpacked the first four *declarative* elements of the gospel in greater detail—God's kingdom is here, Jesus is the Christ, he died for our sins, and he was resurrected on the third day—and now, we turn to consider the imperative elements of Jesus' gospel: repent of sin, believe the gospel, and follow Jesus. Of these, the primary imperative of Jesus' gospel is the call to follow him. From the Bible, we understand that repentance and belief are the first steps of following him. Before we get to repentance and belief, though, let's consider the importance and meaning of two of the most powerful words in all of Scripture: "Follow me."

7

FOLLOW JESUS AND BE SAVED

"There is only one path to final salvation, the path of discipleship....
We are only and ever saved by discipleship to Jesus."

—MATTHEW BATES

The most controversial element of the discipleship gospel is the imperative call to *follow Jesus*. The non-discipleship gospels being preached today do not include *following Jesus* at all—not one of them. As soon as following Jesus becomes an optional add-on to the gospel, it's a death sentence for disciple making. If we're deceived into thinking that following Jesus isn't essential, then we won't do it. The fundamental problem here is that because of the proliferation of non-discipleship gospels, people think they can believe the gospel and be Christians without following Jesus. Nothing could be farther from the truth.

When people say that the call of Jesus' gospel are his words "follow me," they mean that Jesus saves those who follow him—and *only* those who follow. In other words, following Jesus is essential to the gospel and necessary for salvation. Most people won't say it as bluntly as this because they're nervous others will accuse them of teaching works-salvation or abusing God's grace. Neither accusation is true biblically. However, in a Christian culture saturated with non-discipleship gospels, you must be prepared to have people question you about these things and be ready to answer them with gentleness and respect (1 Pet. 3:15).

Pray a Little, One-Time Prayer

This is a standard practice in gospel-preaching churches in America today: a person wanders into a church building, they hear some presentation of the gospel, and they are invited to pray a version of the sinner's prayer. After they've done this, they're told with unwavering confidence that they are "saved." But are they? It seems that the church is doing what singer Dionne Warwick sang in "I Say a Little Prayer" (from the late 1960s) rather than what Jesus taught us to do. Does Jesus ever lead someone into salvation with something that's even remotely like praying the sinner's prayer anywhere in the Gospels? Not even close.

Don't misunderstand us at this point. We're not suggesting that people haven't been truly saved by expressing their faith in Christ through prayer—because they have. We're also not suggesting that prayer isn't a fantastic way to begin following Jesus—because it is. But to think that saying a one-time prayer is the only response to the gospel that Christ calls us to is, in a word, delusional. For starters, praying a one-time prayer in no way reflects the teaching of Jesus. We must stop giving people the impression that it's all the gospel demands of us. Jesus calls us to surrender our whole life to him with the gospel, not just pray a token prayer. Mark shares an account of Jesus saying, "For whoever saves his life will lose it, but *whoever loses his life for my sake and the gospel's will save it*" (Mark 8:35, emphasis ours).

Jesus teaches that those who follow him will enter the kingdom of God and inherit eternal life. While Jesus did, in fact, die to atone for "the sins of the whole world," as 1 John 2:2 says, he also taught that only those who follow him are saved. One of the greatest evangelistic opportunities of Jesus' ministry demonstrates this truth: his encounter with the man known as the rich, young ruler. We now consider this encounter in more detail. Warning: Jesus' words in this story may ruffle your feathers if you're really listening to what he says.

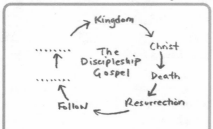

80

Jesus' Great Evangelistic Moment

One of Jesus' most thought-provoking evangelistic moments is found in Mark 10. A man ran up to Jesus, fell to his knees before him, and said, "What must I do to inherit eternal life?" What an amazing evangelistic opportunity, right? Jesus had a prime chance to share the gospel here, but he does something surprising instead. After asking the man a few questions, Jesus answered, "You lack one thing: go, sell all that you have and give to the poor, and you will have treasure in heaven; and come, follow me" (Mark 10:21, ESV). The man didn't do what Jesus told him to do. Instead, he turned his back on Jesus and walked away, sad—and Jesus let him leave.

Wait a minute! What was that?! At first glance, it would seem that Jesus totally blew it. Rather than inviting this man to pray the sinner's prayer, something the man would have no doubt done gladly, Jesus told him to sell all his possessions. What was Jesus doing? Was he advocating works-salvation? Was he adding a legalistic demand to the gospel? By today's "pray-a-little-prayer" standards, it sure sounds like it. Things would have ended so much nicer and neater *for us* if Jesus had done this, but that's not what he did. He called for more. Instead of getting a quick convert, Jesus let the man walk away, back to his large house full of "great possessions" (Mark 10:22).

In the midst of all this, we miss the fact that Jesus told the man exactly what he needed to do to inherit eternal life, just as he'd asked. Jesus told the man to get rid of everything that was more important to him, using the words "follow me." How does one inherit eternal life? By following Jesus. Later in the same chapter, Peter says, "See, we have left everything and followed you" (Mark 10:28). As a result, Jesus assured him and the others that they would, indeed, inherit eternal life in the age to come. What must we do to be saved? According to Jesus, we must repent of our sin, believe in the gospel, *and follow him.*[1]

People struggle to know what to do with Jesus' encounter with the rich man in Mark 10 because they're just not used to having the gospel so closely associated with the cost of discipleship. They're used to hearing that salvation is free, that inheriting eternal life doesn't cost a thing, and that entering God's kingdom is as easy as praying a little prayer. The Bible teaches us that salvation is a gift, to be sure, but not that it's free (Eph. 2:8-10). It cost Jesus his life, and if we follow Jesus, it might cost us our life, too.

Some Christians are so used to having their "ears tickled" by the false promises of non-discipleship gospels that they get gravely offended by anyone who suggests the gospel is calling us to do anything that isn't easy, convenient, or comfortable (2 Tim. 4:3, NASB). Unfortunately, if Jesus said in churches today what he said to the rich, young ruler in his day, people in churches across America today would likely walk away from Jesus, just like the rich young ruler—that's if they didn't try to throw Jesus off a cliff, like those in the Nazareth synagogue (Mark 10:22; Luke 4:29).

If you're going to be part of the solution, you must count the cost of preaching the cost of discipleship. Jesus never left the cost of discipleship in the fine print, as we can see from Mark 10. He made it the headline news. If you start calling people to follow Jesus when you preach the gospel, be prepared. It's likely you'll be peppered with questions insinuating you're teaching works-salvation or that you are impinging on God's grace. At worst, you might be accused of being a false teacher, especially by those who have been caught *hook, line, and sinker* by "gospels" like the forgiveness-only gospel. When we proclaim the gospel of the kingdom, as Jesus did, we must be unafraid to lovingly explain the cost of discipleship. Otherwise, we're presenting the gospel more like a *bait-and-switch*, which Jesus never did.

Sit Down and Count the Cost

When you call people to *follow Jesus* as part of a full gospel presentation, they have an immediate sense that salvation will require more of them than just what happens in that moment; it calls us to a whole new way of life. It's like what Peter and Andrew knew when Jesus said to them: "Follow me, and I will make you become fishers of men" (Mark 1:17, ESV). They knew that at a minimum, Jesus was calling them to leave their fishing business (no small thing) and join him to "fish for men." They knew it was a call to obedience and a new life of following Jesus.

When we include the imperative to *follow Jesus* as an essential element of the gospel, it should give people pause for one of two reasons. Either they aren't used to hearing the call to follow Jesus as part of the gospel, or alternatively, they will realize the potential price to pay for believing the gospel and they begin counting the cost. This is exactly how Christ intended it. Jesus said, "Whoever does not take up his cross and come after me cannot be my disciple" (Luke 14:27). Then, in the very next verse, Jesus told everyone listening in the crowd to "sit down and count the cost" (14:28).

It's important to note here that Jesus said this to the "great crowds" who gathered around him (14:25). As such, he wasn't teaching his closest disciples about the cost of discipleship; he taught the crowds because he wanted everyone to know the cost and count it. This is like other "high cost" calls to discipleship, including the following:

- "And a scribe came up and said to him, 'Teacher, I will follow you wherever you go.' And Jesus said to him, 'Foxes have holes, and birds of the air have nests, but the Son of Man has nowhere to lay his head.' Another of the disciples said to him, 'Lord, let me first go and bury my father.' And Jesus said to him, 'Follow me, and leave the dead to bury their own dead'" (Matt. 19-22).
- "The one who endures to the end will be saved" (Matt. 24:13).
- "If anyone comes to me and does not hate his own father and mother and wife and children and brothers and sisters, yes, even his own life, he cannot be my disciple" (Luke 14:25-27).
- "So, therefore, any one of you who does not renounce all that he has cannot be my disciple" (Luke 14:33).
- "If they persecuted me, they will also persecute you" (John 15:20).

These examples where Jesus addresses the "cost of discipleship" take place in front of the crowds, just as with the rich, young ruler. He wanted everyone to be aware of the price they might have to pay for following him so they could count that cost before saying "yes." These examples also help us grasp that Jesus is calling us to follow him with neither condition nor excuses—to the end. There was no "one foot in, one foot out" discipleship for Jesus. The call of his gospel is ultimately an *all or nothing* type of thing. As we write this, we can hear some people yelling, "They're teaching works-salvation!" It's not. Let us explain.

This Is Not "Works-Salvation"

If you've spent any length of time in a Bible-teaching church, chances are you've got an ultra-sensitive works-salvation detector. If someone sounds like they're trying to add an unbiblical requirement or some sort of legalistic demand to the gospel, an alarm goes off in your head. This is good. It's good to be on the lookout for false gospels, especially legalistic add-ons. That is, unless your radar is misinformed. An ultra-sensitive works-salvation detector can actually be harmful if it causes us to think an essential element of the gospel, like following Jesus, is works-salvation.

Is calling people to *follow Jesus* works-salvation? This is an important question because it cuts to the very heart of God's amazing grace, not to mention our understanding of the gospel. We need to be crystal clear on the answer here; otherwise, people will dismiss Jesus' gospel as a works-salvation gospel, which it is not. Rightly understood, following Jesus is always and only the work of the Holy Spirit. No one is able to follow Jesus without the Holy Spirit, and the Holy Spirit is God's gift to us. How, then, can following Jesus be works-salvation? How can something we do by God's grace be works-salvation? It can't be, and it isn't. To say that "it's done by God's grace" is the same as saying, "we're doing it *in the power of his Holy Spirit*," because the Holy Spirit is a gift of God's grace to us.

Following Jesus is the work of God in our lives, nothing less. Paul admonished us: "Work out your own salvation with fear and trembling, *for it is God who works in you*, both to will and to work for his good pleasure"

(Phil. 2:12-13, emphasis ours). Following Jesus isn't *us working for* our salvation; it is *God working out* salvation in us! Some people will object: "But I can follow Jesus in my own strength, without the Holy Spirit!" The truth is *no, you can't*, at least not according to the Bible. Following Jesus *in your own strength* is not actually following Jesus.[2] It's a work of the flesh. Following Jesus happens only and always in the power of the Spirit. This isn't tricky semantics; it's biblical theology. Calling people to follow Jesus isn't *adding* something extra to the gospel; it's *restoring* an essential element of it.

Good Works Are Not Bad

We did a study regarding "works" in the New Testament for this book, and we found all sorts of "works," including:

- Works of the flesh
- Works of the law
- Unfruitful works
- Works of darkness
- Evil works
- Dead works
- Works apart from faith
- Good works

From this list, only *good works* are considered good. The other seven kinds of works listed above can be categorized as "bad," meaning they are sinful works of the flesh. We know that our own works don't save us because of verses like Ephesians 2:8-9: "For by grace you have been saved through faith. And this is not your own doing, it is the gift of God, *not a result of works,* so that no one may boast" (emphasis ours). The Apostle Paul's point is clear: we are saved by grace through faith. In other words, we're saved by God's work on our behalf, not our own works (any of the first seven *works* on the list above). In stating this, though, we must be very careful not to throw in "good works" with all the other "bad" works. In the Bible, good works are never described as *bad*—ever.

Being saved by grace, as Ephesians 2:8-9 teaches us, involves continuing to live in grace. God's grace doesn't stop with conversion; it continues seamlessly as we grow into disciples. Essentially, we live in grace the rest of our lives. A concept of God's grace that converts but is disconnected from discipleship is woefully weak (not to mention unbiblical). Many Christians don't think about discipleship as living in God's grace; they think of discipleship as an unnecessary add-on, something optional. At worst, they think a gospel that demands discipleship is a "works-salvation" gospel. But can you be living in God's grace and not be living a life of discipleship?

It's not enough to read Ephesians 2:8-9; we must read Ephesians 2:10 with it, as well. In this verse, Paul teaches us God's purpose for saving us *by grace through faith,* and it has to do with good works. Verse 10 says, "For we are his workmanship, created in Christ Jesus *for good works,* which God prepared beforehand, that we should walk *in them*" (emphasis ours). We're not saved *by works,* but God has saved us *for good works.* More than that, God himself has prepared these good works for us, and he also calls us to "walk in them."

To walk in the good works that God has prepared for us is to follow Jesus in the power of the Holy Spirit. If we really let this sink in, we realize good works are the good fruit of abiding in Christ (John 15:7-8). At this point, take note: there is not one verse in Jesus' teaching (or in his apostles' teaching) that says good works are bad. Jesus said that he did good works. He also taught that his followers would do good works, too. In fact, he said they would do not just *good* works but *great* works: "Truly, truly, I say to you, whoever believes in me will also do the works that I do; and *greater* works than these will he do, because I am going to the Father" (John 14:12, emphasis ours). God has been doing good works from the beginning, starting with his acts in creation.

God Does Good Works

The first mention of "good works" in the Bible is a reference to God's work in creation. For six days, the Bible says, God created the heavens and the earth (Gen. 1). This creative activity is defined as "work" in the Bible—God's work (Gen. 2:2). When he had completed his work of creation, he pronounced all his work to be "good," and more than that, "very good" (Gen. 1:31). We can glean from this "first mention" of good works in the Bible that first, good works aren't bad, and second, that good works are the mighty work of God![3]

Just as God did good work in creation, he is doing a good work in everyone who follows Jesus, making them into a new creation in Christ (2 Cor. 5:17). In Philippians 1:6, Paul promises us that, "he who began a good work in you will bring it to completion on the day of Christ Jesus." Knowing this brings us to the precipice of truly *living in* God's grace, not just being *saved by* it. We no longer have to be afraid that being obedient to Christ and loving others (both *good works*) are bad or unrighteous or works of the flesh. Rather, we're free to focus on the "greater works" that Jesus said we, as his followers, would do and that God has prepared in advance for us to walk in (John 14:12; Eph. 2:10). This is how the German theologian Dietrich Bonhoeffer understood following Jesus.

Dietrich Bonhoeffer and Following Jesus

Dietrich Bonhoeffer is often celebrated by the American church because of his life's story, but we don't really know much about his actual teaching. We admire him for standing up as a Christian to Adolf Hilter and the Third Reich during World War II and for being killed in a Nazi concentration camp for it, but what do we really know of his teachings? We like Bonhoeffer's story, but have we really listened to what he said?

If we were able to ask Dietrich Bonhoeffer whether following Jesus is works-salvation, he'd reply with an emphatic *Nien!* (German for "no"). He might, then, open up his book, *The Cost of Discipleship*, and read from the chapter titled "Grace and Discipleship":

> Grace is *costly* because it calls us to follow, and it is *grace* because it calls us to follow *Jesus Christ*. It is costly because it costs a man his life, and it is grace because it gives a man the only true life. It is costly because

it condemns sin, and grace because it justifies the sinner. Above all, it is *costly* because it cost God the life of his Son: "ye were bought at a price," and what has cost God much cannot be cheap for us.[4]

At some point, Bonhoeffer might stop reading, look us straight in the eyes through his wiry glasses, and tell us that our question about whether following Jesus is works-salvation indicates we had sold-out to "cheap grace" as he called it in the same book. He would say that following Jesus isn't works-salvation at all—it's a part of salvation itself! This realization could cause some people who say they like Bonhoeffer to question whether they still do or not. Like Jesus, we shouldn't admire Bonhoeffer's life without also considering his words.

A New Bonhoeffer Generation

We've found that the focus on following Jesus in *The Cost of Discipleship* is striking a cord with a new generation of American pastors and ministry leaders. They have grown up in the era of church with all the bells and whistles. No matter what these leaders have done, there's always some church doing it bigger and better down the street. They have felt the pressure to "put on a show" every Sunday morning, but they are sick and tired of having their ministry judged by others (and themselves!) according to the rise and fall of attendance and how much money people put in the offering plate each week.

We see a new generation of women and men in the church who are repenting of preaching a cheap-grace, non-discipleship gospel that avoids calling people to follow Jesus and rarely mentions the cost of discipleship. We see this new generation of leaders in our work with The Bonhoeffer Project. They are learning to call people to follow Jesus no matter the cost, without conditions, without excuses, until the end—just as Bonhoeffer did.

We must include the call to follow Jesus in our preaching of the gospel. When we do, it's a full-frontal attack on the false promises associated with non-discipleship gospels. It helps people grasp the fact that salvation is not a one-time decision, but rather a call to live a new life. It also gives them a sense that there is a cost associated with believing the gospel, a cost they need to count according to Jesus. The church needs to recover this essential element of the gospel in its preaching. But for this to happen fully, we need to restore our understanding of repentance and belief, which is what we're focusing on in the next chapter.

8

REPENT AND BELIEVE THE GOSPEL

"The Gospel is protected by the preaching of repentance
which calls sin sin and declares the sinner guilty."

—Dietrich Bonhoeffer

The gospel demands a response from us, which is the call to follow Jesus. Our savior was unmistakably clear about how we are to start following him: "Repent and believe in the gospel" (Mark 1:15). As we learned earlier in Part 1, both repentance and belief are essential elements of Jesus' gospel. Rightly understood, repentance and belief are *the first steps* of following Jesus (and the first steps of many). In other words, our conversion should be marked by repentance and belief, but so should the rest of our lives.

Despite the importance of repentance and belief in Scripture, you wouldn't know it by how we treat these elements. Repentance has become a questionable element of the gospel in our day, and belief in Jesus has been watered down. If we operate on the basis of a diluted understanding of biblical repentance and belief, the rest of the discipleship gospel will be almost incomprehensible. That's why in this chapter we'll delve deeper into the importance and meaning of these two elements, seeking to fortify them as essential to the gospel once again. Before we do, though, we need to establish a strong, expositional connection between repentance, belief, and following Jesus.

Following Jesus, Repentance, and Belief

When some people read through Mark 1:14-17, as we did in Part 1, they might object that Jesus' call to *follow* (v. 17) is separate and distinct from his call to *repent* and *believe* the gospel (v. 15). They might argue that verse 15 is a different geographical setting from verse 17—and they'd be right. In verse 15, Jesus is proclaiming the gospel and calling people to repent and believe. Then, in verse 16, the geographical setting apparently changes, indicated by the words, "Passing along the Sea of Galilee." So, the argumentation of some would say that Jesus' call to *follow* in verse 17 *isn't* connected to verse 15 and, as such, following Jesus *isn't* an essential element of Jesus' gospel. While a first reading of this verse might seem like this is the case, a deeper consideration shows us the opposite. There are at least two solid, expositional reasons for this.

First, Jesus calls us to *follow* him in a different geographical setting than his call to *repent* and *believe*. However, he gives these three calls in close literary context to one another. This observation is important because being within the same immediate context to each other serves to bring together the calls of verse 15—to repent and believe—with the call to follow in verse 17. As such, Mark helps us understand what it means to repent and believe (1:15) by giving us a specific example in verse 17, where Andrew and Simon leave everything to follow Jesus. In other words, what does it look like to repent and believe? It looks like the regular life of following Jesus. Alternatively, how do we begin following Jesus? We repent of our sin and believe in the gospel.

A second piece of expositional evidence connecting Jesus' call to *follow* in Mark 1:17 to his calls to *repent* and *believe* (v. 15) is a technical, grammatical one. It has to do with the word "and", which begins Mark 1:16. It's not always translated in English (which is the case with the *English Standard Version* of the Bible that we cited above). But in all the oldest and best Greek manuscripts of Mark's Gospel, the word "and" does exist at the beginning of Mark 1:16.

Why is this important? The Greek word *kai* (translated "and") is a Greek *connective* word. The writer, Mark, is intentionally seeking to connect what happened in verse 15 (repent, believe) to what comes after it in verse 17 (follow) by purposefully placing the connective word "and" at the beginning of verse 16. So, not only is Jesus' call to *follow* in the immediate context of his calls to *repent* and *believe*, but Mark has also purposefully connected these three imperative responses together. Now that we have established a strong expositional connection between the three imperative calls of the gospel, let's consider the essential nature of repentance to the gospel.

Repentance is Radical

The word "repent" involves the idea of a radical change of mind *and heart*. Specifically, it describes a person once living in unbelief, disobedience, and even disdain for the things of God, and then, post-conversion, living with belief, obedience, and love for God. The change is radical. Our friend, Greg Ogden, author of *Transformational Discipleship*, calls repentance "a crisis word."[1] It's a *crisis* in the best possible sense. It's the first sign that the gospel has truly taken hold of a person's life, the first fruits of following Jesus.

Jesus often put the importance of repentance into sharp perspective in his teaching. For example, in Luke 13:3, he said, "Unless you repent, you will all likewise perish." After declaring this, he repeated himself—word for word—just two verses later. His point was strong and serious: those who don't repent *will perish*, meaning that they will die apart from Christ in this life, and they will also be separated from him for all eternity in a state of judgment and punishment (Matt. 25:46).

As we've already seen, Jesus made it crystal clear that repentance was an essential element of the gospel the very first time he preached the gospel (Mark 1:15)! It was also a critical aspect of the apostles' gospel proclamation. Paul, for instance, while preaching in Athens, proclaimed: "Now [God] commands all people everywhere to repent" (Acts 17:30). Paul included everyone in this call to repent. In other words, we all need to repent.

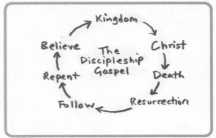

Despite the fact that Jesus and the apostles' teaching is black and white on this issue, a fog of grey has descended upon the church today with respect to whether or not repentance is critical to the gospel.

Is Repentance Really Necessary?

Many in our day doubt whether or not it's necessary to repent of sin for salvation. This doubt indicates just how far we've drifted from the gospel that Jesus preached. When you listen to many gospel presentations and read most gospel tracts today, they deal lightly with repentance, if at all. The proliferation of non-discipleship gospels in the American church has resulted in the removal of repentance from the gospel.

We see a variety of explanations for this. First, repentance deals with sin. Preachers of non-discipleship gospels, such as the consumer gospel, don't talk much about sin, so they leave repentance out, too. Second, some theological systems parse out repentance from the gospel, arguing that it was for Old Testament Israel, but it isn't for the New Testament church. Third, there are those who view repentance as an unnecessary burden, a needless obstacle, "trouble" for those ready to believe.[2] Fourth, some understand repentance as a "work of the flesh," something we do in our own strength. This renders repentance not only unnecessary, but an assault on God's grace, according to them.

In light of Jesus' teaching and the apostles' writings on repentance, these anti-repentance arguments seem absurd. A gospel without repentance—even a diluted version of repentance—is a gospel that neither Jesus nor his apostles preached. However, anti-repentance advocates have spread like a viral outbreak throughout churches in America in recent times. It's one of the reasons that disciple making in local churches is on life support in many locations (if it hasn't already flatlined). We haven't contained these non-discipleship gospels with their anti-repentance emphasis either. Rather, we've exported them at a rapid rate! We've sent them around the world through missions.

Exporting Anti-Repentance

The American church has been one of the greatest missionary forces for the spread of the gospel in the history of the church. Thousands of missionaries have been sent to the far corners of the earth with the gospel from the United States. But what if the gospel these missionaries have been taking into the whole world isn't the gospel that Jesus preached? What if hundreds, maybe even thousands, of our missionaries have gone out with a non-discipleship gospel infected with an anti-repentance emphasis? We believe that many of them may have, thus propagating a false gospel. We know of a mission organization that sends out hundreds of people into the world every year to share "the gospel" with others who have never heard the name of Jesus. This would be great, except that behind closed doors this organization threatened to remove one of their leaders if he continued to include repentance in his gospel training. This massive mission organization doesn't want their missionaries mentioning repentance at all as part of their "gospel" presentation.

Is a gospel without repentance consistent with Jesus' gospel? Plain and simple: *no*. A gospel without the essential element of repentance is a non-discipleship gospel. Likewise, if lost sinners haven't been called to repent of their sin, can we really say they've heard the gospel Jesus preached? Again, the answer is *no*. There is an urgent need to restore biblical repentance to the gospel in the American church today because we have a global missional influence.

The Reformation and Repentance

As we write this book, celebrations of the five hundredth anniversary of the Reformation are just coming to end. The Reformation famously began in 1517 with Martin Luther nailing "The 95 Theses" to the door of the church at Wittenberg. It's significant that the *very first of the ninety-five* had to do with repentance. Luther wrote: "When our Lord and Master Jesus Christ said 'Repent,' he intended that the entire life of believers should be repentance." We seem to have lost this impetus as Protestants. Luther wasn't crying out for some weak, flimsy version of repentance. His call was for the restoration of true, biblical repentance.

Luther's words should cause us to think. As we've been saying, some Christians consider repentance *unnecessary* for salvation. There are others who, while they think repentance *is necessary* for salvation, they only think of it as a one-time decision at conversion. This isn't what Luther described either. True, biblical repentance isn't just part of "getting saved"; it's part of the daily life of a disciple that impacts "the entire life of believers." In other words, repentance is critical at conversion, but also throughout our life as disciples.

The Reformation happened five hundred years ago, and it quite literally began with a call for a revival of repentance in the church. Five hundred years later, it would seem we need another reformation. Like its predecessor, this new reformation also needs to begin with reviving true, biblical repentance to the gospel.

True, Biblical Repentance

Left to ourselves, we *won't* repent; really, we *can't* repent without the Spirit. Jesus said, "When [the Holy Spirit] comes, He will convict the world of sin and righteousness and judgment" (John 16:10). Actually, there is a sense in which repentance is the work of the Trinity. God the Father gives the Holy Spirit to energize repentance in us, which, in turn, empowers us to follow Jesus. Since repentance is the work of God in us, no one can boast about repentance or take credit for repenting or think they are "holy than thou" because of their repentance. God receives all the praise for one sinner who repents.

The Apostle Paul teaches us about repentance in 2 Corinthians 7:10 when he writes, "For godly grief produces a repentance that leads to salvation without regret, whereas worldly grief produces death." Paul teaches us in this verse that *godly grief* produces repentance that leads to salvation and *worldly grief* does not. Aldous Huxley, an agnostic who often ridiculed Christianity, understood this fake, worldly grief that masquerades as repentance. Huxley vividly described it as "rolling in the muck," which he recognized was "a most undesirable sentiment."[3] Unfortunately, these words of Huxley demonstrate that he understood repentance better than some Christians today.

It's important to notice that Paul teaches us that repentance leads to salvation in 2 Corinthians 7:10. Did you notice that? He states that "godly grief produces a repentance *that leads to salvation*" (emphasis ours). Pay careful attention to these words. If the case that repentance is an essential element of the gospel wasn't already strong enough, these words only serve to put it beyond the shadow of a doubt. In fact, they make it crystal clear that a person cannot be saved if they do not repent of sin.

Repentance and Belief

Like two sides of the same coin, repentance and belief go together. They are the *first steps* of following Jesus. While we can distinguish between these two elements, we shouldn't sever or separate repentance from belief in our minds. (This is one of the reasons we're addressing both of these elements in one chapter—to reinforce this point!) You can't repent and *not believe*. Likewise, you can't believe if you don't repent.

As we transition from a discussion of repentance to a consideration of belief, we need to acknowledge how the two are intricately intertwined. As we repent of our sin, there is a clear sense in Scripture that we're turning *away from our sin* and turning *toward Christ*—to believe in him. When Jesus called people to "repent and believe in the gospel," that is what he meant. In other words, you can't do one of them without the other. Keep this connection in mind as we dig deeper into true, biblical belief.

What Amazed Jesus?

The Bible records two things that amazed Jesus while he was on earth. It's an amazing thing that Jesus was amazed by anything in this world, for he created all things in it (Col. 1:16)! Nevertheless, we're told that two things amazed him: *belief* and *lack of it*. He was amazed at a Roman centurion's *belief* in Luke 7, but he was also amazed at the *unbelief* of those in his own hometown of Nazareth in Mark 6. The fact that the Gospel writers highlight how amazing *belief* and *unbelief* were to Jesus should cause us to consider whether or not this belief amazes us.

Not only was Jesus amazed by belief, he also went out of his way to highlight it. For example, he highlighted a woman's belief in Mark 5, who was healed of previously incurable bleeding. We're told that power went out of Jesus and that she was healed instantly. Jesus said to her for the entire crowd to hear, "Daughter, *your faith* has made you well" (Mark 5:34, emphasis ours). This presents us with a beautiful yet theologically complex situation. She was healed—that's the beautiful part! But was it by *his power* or *her belief* that made her well? Jesus said it was *her belief*, which is fascinating, and we mustn't discount the Son of God's words. According to Jesus, belief in him is powerful.

The Call to Believe

While the Gospels give us numerous accounts of how Jesus constantly called people to *repent, believe,* and *follow* him, it's rare to find all three of these imperative gospel calls together. What we find, instead, is Jesus calling people to either repent *or* believe *or* follow him. This might be confusing until we understand the cultural and religious context into which he spoke. In our study of the Gospels, we have found that Jesus called people to *repent* in response to the gospel (more than 25 times); other times, he called them to *follow* (more than 80 references); but most often, he called people to *believe* (more than 125 examples). While the gospel calls us to respond fully, Jesus proclaimed the gospel with a freedom to call people to respond to it in one or all of these ways.

The way Jesus spoke about these three elements reveals two lessons about the imperative thrust of the gospel. First, when he called people to respond to the gospel, he sometimes used all three calls; other times, he used only one of them. Here's the crux, though. When he called with one, *the others were implied* (more on this below). Second, the call to believe was Jesus' dominant gospel call in the sense that he used it the most often. All three calls are imperative, but belief was dominant in Jesus' preaching.

Nicodemus as a Test Case for Belief

One of Jesus' famous calls to believe was during his interactions with Nicodemus in John 3. Jesus spoke of believing with Nicodemus three times before the well-known declaration of John 3:16, which also calls people to believe. When Jesus called Nicodemus to believe, he understood, due to his Jewish background, that believing in him went hand-in-hand with repentance from sin and following him. In fact, this is most likely why Nicodemus struggled to believe—because he knew the scope of the call! Nicodemus was not only Jewish but also a Pharisee. For him, *believing* in Jesus meant that he had to "repent" of his legalistic ways as a Pharisee and begin literally following Jesus in public as one of his disciples (Matt. 23:13-15).

Believing in Jesus would have radically and very practically changed Nicodemus's life. He knew that to believe in Jesus meant he could no longer officially be a Pharisee, which would've triggered other major changes in his life, like being ostracized by the Pharisees, possibly being expelled from the synagogue, and even being rejected by his family for bringing shame upon them (John 9:22). Nicodemus knew the high cost of believing in Jesus because his belief necessarily included his repentance and discipleship. He is a clear example of how Jesus' call to believe implies and involves repentance and discipleship.

We don't read about Nicodemus again until we see him at Christ's death (John 20:39) and realize that Nicodemus was following Jesus even at the time of his crucifixion. To follow Jesus at the time when Jesus was put to death was to put your own life at risk—an indication that he really had repented and believed in Jesus, that he had truly been "born again." Nicodemus had left his old life behind and was following Jesus—no matter the cost, without conditions, and without excuses.

Powerless Gift-Card Belief

Today, belief is being drained of its power in a growing number of churches. You don't need to believe in much to believe in many of the non-discipleship gospels being preached! Modern-day belief can have an appearance of godliness, but it lacks power to change someone's life (2 Tim. 3:5). This phenomenon of *powerless belief* might have something to do with the fact that we no longer understand belief as a life-transforming force that opens our eyes to God and leads us to surrender everything for Jesus. Instead, we've come to think of it like receiving a gift card. When you receive a gift card, you have the opportunity to get stuff—whatever you want. This is how many people think of salvation today.

Gift-card belief says, *If I believe in the gospel, then I get stuff from God!* We get forgiveness, we get to go to heaven, and we don't need a life change— not one little bit. Gift-card belief doesn't require repentance and isn't connected to discipleship at all. For people with gift-card belief, obedience isn't necessary, discipleship is optional, and displaying the fruit of the Spirit is just for "serious Christians." To require such things as necessary for salvation is equivalent to waging war on God's grace (or so they've been taught). Something's amiss here. In the name of "God's grace," belief has become powerless and passive in the church.

Abram Went

In contrast with gift-card belief, biblical belief is actionable, beyond mental ascent. It's about trusting Jesus in ways that cause you to *do things you would never do* if you were not following him. Abram understood this. When God told Abram to leave his home in Ur in Genesis 12 and go to an undefined land that he would show him, the Bible simply says, "Abram went" (Genesis 12:4). American scholar Thomas Cahill, a man with unusual insight, wrote that "these are two of the boldest words in all literature."[4] Abram did what God asked him to do. He listened to God, trusted him, and did what God said. In the Bible, that's called belief. Because Abram did what God said, he is highlighted as one of the great examples of *belief* in the Bible (Heb. 11:9). Abram gives us an example of how belief isn't passive, it's active. When God says something, true belief acts on it—obeying and doing what God says.

The lack of disciple making in churches today (and the passivity it perpetuates) betrays a deficient understanding of belief. Christians have convinced themselves that they believe in disciple making, even though they're not making disciples. To be fair, they've been taught that going to church and giving money *is* making disciples. If you trace the problem all the way to its source—which is an insufficient theology of the gospel—Christians today think they can believe in Jesus without acting on it. But this isn't the belief Abram exemplified, and it's not the belief that amazed Jesus, either. It's powerless, unbiblical belief that won't save a soul. If we truly believed in disciple making, we would be making disciples, not excuses.

Issuing the Full Call of the Gospel

In light of this weak, powerless understanding of belief, don't just call people to believe the gospel. Rather, call them to *repent* of sin, *believe* the gospel, and *follow* Jesus. When you preach the gospel, it's a best practice to use all three imperative calls of the gospel, not just one like belief, for example. Use the *full* call of the gospel, as Jesus modeled for us in Mark 1:14-17. If you do this, watch the changes that begin to happen. People will start grasping how the gospel is calling them to respond—to be multiplying disciples on mission with Jesus, not just aimless church attendees wandering through life.

As you read that last paragraph, those of you who have been paying close attention might raise your hand and exclaim, "But you just got finished telling us how powerful biblical belief is and that Jesus himself called people to believe more than one hundred and twenty-five times!" That's true, we did. We're not Jesus, though. Even more to the point, we're not living in the first century anymore. There is a stark contrast between Jesus' day and today as it relates to understanding the call of the gospel.

The Full Gospel Call

In Jesus' day, there were many people like Nicodemus, people who understood that belief is comprehensive, powerful, and amazing—and leads people to do what Jesus commanded. People in Jesus' day also understood that repentance and discipleship were implied and included in the call to believe, but this isn't the case today. Most people today have no idea of what the Bible means when it calls us to *believe the gospel*. As heralds of the gospel, we need to help them fill in the blanks. A practical and powerful way to do this is by issuing the *full* call of the gospel—to repent, believe, and follow Jesus.

Belief in the Bible is powerful. Nowadays, there are a lot of cheap, powerless imitations of it. There is a lot of "gift-card belief" around, which might look like biblical belief, sound like it, and pretend to be it, but it's not. You can tell over time by the untransformed, fruitless life of the person who professes it. Belief caused Abram to follow God to a foreign land, it led Nicodemus to follow Jesus to his crucifixion, and it has the power to amaze Jesus. We need to resuscitate this kind of belief in the church—the kind of belief that's energized by repentance and follows Christ to the end.

PART THREE

THE DISCIPLES WE MAKE

In this next section, we hope to bring the whole book together for you. Remember all the ground we've covered already in the first two parts. In Part 1, we considered the nature of the gospel Jesus preached during his public ministry on earth. We noted the four declarative statements of Jesus' gospel: God's kingdom is here, he is the Christ, he died for our sins, and he was resurrected from the dead. We designated these four declarations as "the gospel proper"—the main declaration of the Good News—and we also looked at the three imperative responses to Jesus' gospel in his preaching—repent of sin, believe the gospel, and follow Jesus. Altogether, we observed seven essential elements of Jesus' gospel, which he called "the gospel of the kingdom of God."

In Part 2, we went deeper into the importance and meaning of each of these seven gospel elements, where we learned the nature of God's kingdom and how a robust understanding of it is essential to the gospel and empowers disciple making. We also discovered how Jesus' identity as the Christ, his death, and his resurrection are all critical aspects of the coming of God's kingdom. These elements also lead us into the major call of the gospel—to follow Jesus, which begins with repentance and belief. The gospel doesn't just *lead to* discipleship; discipleship (following Jesus) is also an essential element of the gospel. That's why we're calling the gospel Jesus preached *the discipleship gospel*. We use this language because of the necessity of emphasizing discipleship in gospel proclamation today.

Now, as we move into Part 3, these multiple threads come together. We'll look at how disciple making today must begin by proclaiming the gospel Jesus preached, which calls us not only to *be* disciples, but also to *make* disciples. As part of this, we want to offer you a definition of the discipleship gospel, essentially a succinct summary of all seven elements in narrative form. After this, we'll discover how proclaiming the discipleship gospel actually leads to disciple making in the church, indeed throughout the whole world. Part 1 gave us the skeleton of the discipleship gospel, Part 2 put flesh on the bones, and now, in Part 3, our goal is to describe how the discipleship gospel can bring disciple making to life for you and the people in your ministry context. As you read, keep in mind our two major assumptions: 1) you cannot make Christlike disciples from a non-discipleship gospel, and 2) the gospel you preach determines the disciples you make.

9

FINALLY! A GOSPEL DEFINITION

"The gospel has been described as a pool in which a
toddler can wade and yet an elephant can swim. It is both
simple enough to tell a child and profound enough for the
greatest minds to explore."

—TIM KELLER

Having a clear definition of the gospel is critical for the church today. We
cannot underscore this enough. One of the reasons for so much confusion about the gospel today is that we haven't clearly defined it. The blank
stares you get if you dare to ask Christians the simple question of "What is
the gospel?" should convince you of this. The church in America doesn't
know the gospel with clarity and conviction, which is primarily a problem
of definition, if anything. We're not arguing that your definition needs to be
exactly like ours, as we describe below; we simply mean that we need clarity
today on the gospel and having an actual, literal definition is the best way
we've found for helping people clarify their understanding of it.

Until we define the gospel by actually writing it down, we can't know
for sure whether the gospel we believe in and share with others is actually
the gospel Jesus preached—or something else. Dallas Willard identifies what

it will take to bring back an understanding of discipleship to the gospel: "It would primarily be a work of scriptural interpretation and theological reformulation, but modification of time-hardened practices will also be required. Radical changes in what we do in the way of 'church' will have to be made."[1] In this chapter, we define the gospel on the foundation of "scriptural interpretation" and "theological reformulation" we have already laid down. We specifically and succinctly answer the question, *What is the gospel?* In the next chapter, we'll discuss some of the "radical changes" that must be made to recover disciple making as the primary practice of the church.

The Word "Gospel"

In ancient times, the word for "gospel" was used to describe an announcement of victory or celebration heralded through the streets for all to hear, making it a declaration (Ps. 96:3). In fact, the word "gospel" literally means "Good News," which is the declaration of a good event. This helps us make sense of why insightful scholars like Scot McKnight speak of the gospel being "a narrative declaration" about Jesus.[2] The gospel is a Scripture-based declaration about who Jesus is, what he has done, how he fulfills Scripture prophecies, and how we should respond to him. We've crafted our gospel definition as a narrative declaration, a story-based paragraph, very similar to 1 Corinthians 15:3-4 but expanded to include all seven essential elements.

To prepare the way for our gospel definition, first we need to address two issues that will set our definition in the right context. The first issue has to do with the necessity for defining the gospel. Is it necessary? If it is, why is it necessary to define it afresh now? The second issue has to do with the consequences of *not* defining the gospel. What might happen if we don't have a clear definition? We begin with the necessity for defining the gospel in the first place.

Isn't The Gospel Already Defined?

As we prepare to define the gospel, some might argue that the gospel has already been defined in the Bible in multiple ways. This is true, but only to a certain extent. For starters, the Bible reveals the gospel throughout all Scripture—every inspired word from Genesis to Revelation.[3] As Jesus told the two disciples on their way to Emmaus after his resurrection, *all* Scripture concerns him (Luke 24:27). Plus, the gospel is revealed through the four Gospels of the New Testament. The Gospels are called such because they reveal the gospel. Not to mention that the gospel is defined in specific passages like 1 Corinthians 15:3-4.[4] These gospel revelations define it in the most primal sense. They are the first written record of a gospel definition in history.

Revelations of the gospel in the Bible do not confront the specific *gospel issues* we're experiencing in much of the contemporary church today, even if they are similar to first-century issues. In stating this, we're not calling into question the sufficiency of Scripture at all! We are questioning, though, whether or not the church's ears have become dull to Jesus' gospel in favor of "gospels" of our own creation—non-discipleship gospels that tickle our ears in various ways rather than confront us with the actual Christ (2 Tim. 4:3).

If Christians today aren't intentionally making disciples—and the majority of them are not—it's not God's fault because he has given us *everything* we need. The reason we're not making disciples today is rooted in the fact that we have not paid close enough attention to Jesus' gospel. We have discipleship deafness, meaning that we no longer hear Jesus' call to *be disciples and to make disciples* as a part of the gospel. As a result, we no longer think that discipleship is part of salvation. Matthew Bates writes, "There is only one path to final salvation, the path of discipleship.... We are only and ever saved by discipleship to Jesus."[5] This is why it's critical to define the gospel today—so that we can hear it again! It's why we call this *the discipleship gospel*—so we can hear Jesus' old gospel anew and with unplugged ears.

In Chapter 2, we identified the five non-discipleship gospels. While these gospels are misguided, make no mistake: these non-discipleship gospels have been clearly defined. In fact, this is one reason their influence is so pervasive in churches and why churches aren't making disciples. Certain tenets of these false gospels are almost considered to be doctrine—that's how bad it has become!

With this in mind (and before we define the discipleship gospel), let's be fully aware of the grave danger

> ### Different Gospels
>
> 1. Forgiveness Only
> 2. Gospel of Left
> 3. Prosperity
> 4. Consumer
> 5. Gospel of Right

of believing and sharing non-discipleship gospels. To fully grasp the problem, we need to know the consequences of not defining the real gospel. The Apostle Paul made the consequences crystal clear to the churches in the region of Galatia: if you don't believe the real gospel, you'll quickly drift into believing and sharing "a different gospel." If that happens, the consequence

'll be cursed! Let's take a closer look at this message and contextu-
alize ~~~ our culture today.

Warning: The Galatian Curse

It's one thing to talk about non-discipleship gospels and how they don't
make Christlike disciples, but it's another thing to realize there's a biblical
curse on those who believe and share "different gospels." The mood gets a lot
more solemn when you start talking about curses, and people also get a lot
more interested in knowing the true gospel. The churches in ancient Galatia
had been infiltrated by men who travelled from church to church sharing a
legalistic and twisted gospel (strains of it are still being preached today; see
"Gospel of the Right" above).[6]

The words you're about to read aren't wishy-washy, sugarcoated, or po-
litically correct. Paul hit these preachers right between the eyes as the Holy
Spirit inspired him. In Galatians 1:6-9, he wrote:

> I am astonished that you are so quickly deserting him who called you in
> the grace of Christ and are turning to a different gospel—not that there
> is another one, but there are some who trouble you and want to distort
> the gospel of Christ. But even if we or an angel from heaven should
> preach to you a gospel contrary to the one we preached to you, let him
> be accursed. As we have said before, so now I say again: If anyone is
> preaching to you a gospel contrary to the one you received, let him be
> accursed. (ESV)

Wow! Not just once but twice, Paul pronounces a curse on these
"gospel" preachers. That's a double-curse! He was serious, and we should
read his inspired words very seriously. The language he uses is stunning. Not
only did he pronounce a double-curse on these preachers, but he also said
that they had *deserted* Christ and *turned away* from grace! If that wasn't severe enough, later in Galatians, he emphatically stated that those who believed in "a different gospel" had been "severed from Christ" and had "fallen
away from grace" (Gal. 5:4).

You may be tempted to turn a blind eye to these strong, uncomfortable,
apostolic words, but resist the temptation. Don't skip over this warning passage, don't dumb it down or explain it away, and don't tell yourself, "Oh,
God wouldn't do that now. Paul just got a little too excited." Let's be clear:

the double-curse on *preaching* a different gospel didn't die with the apostles; it applies today just the same. Neither did the consequences of *believing* a different gospel die; those too are very real realities for many people today.

If a person preaches "a different gospel" in the twenty-first century, they have the same apostolic double-curse upon them as those in the first century. What's more, that person's converts are "twice as much a child of hell" as they are, according to Jesus![7] This means that we must heed Paul's words and let them sink in. If you do, then you'll pay much closer attention to the gospel you believe and share. You'll also listen more attentively to the gospel in your congregation, and your ears will be opened to hear Jesus' gospel. If we don't listen carefully, the possibility of drifting to a different gospel is far greater—and "a different gospel" leads to the double-curse! Now, the waiting on an answer to the simple question, "What is the gospel?" is over.

Finally, a Definition!

It's time to offer a complete and written definition of the discipleship gospel. Remember, the gospel is a Scripture-based declaration in narrative form that tells us who Jesus is, what he has done, how he fulfills all Scripture, and how he calls us to respond to him. This is the format of our gospel definition. It's structured around the framework of 1 Corinthians 15:3-4, expanded to include all seven elements of Jesus' gospel.

What Is the Gospel?

The gospel is this: *the Kingdom of God* has come through Jesus of Nazareth. He is *Christ*, the King, God's one and only Son. He *died* on the cross for our sins, was buried, and was *resurrected* on the third day according to the Scriptures. In His great love and by His amazing grace, God our Father saves everyone who *repents* of their sin, *believes* the gospel, and *follows* Jesus in the power of the Holy Spirit. When King Jesus returns on the last day, the great Day of Judgment, everyone who followed Him will enter the eternal Kingdom of God.

(Mark 1:14-17; 8:27-31; 1 Cor. 15:1-5; John 3:16; Eph. 2:8-10; Matt. 25:31-46)

Right off the bat, we know this definition isn't "inspired," but we've carefully chosen every word and based each one in Scripture. In fact, each one of the six Scripture references beneath the definition relates directly to specific words and phrases in the definition. We're also not under any delusion that our definition is *the answer*, either, because it's not. It *is* a starting point and one example for you to consider (and potentially use). You may, alternatively, reshape it using other biblical language that is better suited to your ministry context.

As you begin processing this definition, take note that it includes the seven essential elements of Jesus' preaching, and it highlights them in italics and bold. This visually reinforces the importance of each one. It's also succinct—about one hundred words, which means that it's primed for memorization. We've listed some unique characteristics of the definition that are worthy of consideration, too. The definition:

- Begins and ends with the kingdom of God
- Includes the "already but not yet" tension of God's kingdom
- Emphasizes Jesus' humanity: "Jesus of Nazareth"
- Highlights Jesus' deity and exclusivity: "God's one and only Son"
- References the Trinity: Father, Son, and Holy Spirit
- Expresses God's love and grace
- Underscores the empowerment of the Holy Spirit
- Concludes with a focus on the end of time

As you define the gospel for your context, make sure to understand how you can use it to resuscitate life into your congregation, for example. It's not enough to have a definition of the gospel stuffed away in a filing cabinet or in a folder on your computer's desktop. We define the gospel so we can teach it to the church and help them memorize it, live it out, and proclaim it to the world. A gospel declaration clarifies for churches who we are as disciples, what we believe, and the nature of our mission on earth. It must be preached repeatedly from the pulpit, declared boldly at baptisms, agreed upon by every member who joins the church, added to the church's doctrinal statement, and very importantly, members need to be discipled in it.

When a church has a clear gospel declaration, that definition becomes a yardstick for the church. We can measure the gospel we are believing and preaching against the gospel Jesus preached—with its seven essential elements. This makes it an important (and very practical!) safeguard against the wind and waves of different doctrines and non-discipleship gospels (Eph. 4:14).

In the midst of our current gospel crisis, every local church should define the gospel—actually writing it down so that members can be equipped to answer the simple but critical question, *What is the gospel?*

The Defining Characteristic

At this point, we want to focus on a particularly important characteristic of our gospel definition. In fact, we've branded the discipleship gospel based on this one characteristic. The ultimate call of Jesus' gospel is to *follow him*. That's why the operative words of our definition are "follow Jesus." The discipleship gospel makes it clear that Christ's call is nothing less than following him. We have strongly underscored this in the gospel definition above by using "follow" two times in back-to-back references. Our definition calls us to follow Jesus and then emphasizes that only those who do follow Jesus will enter the eternal kingdom of God, just as Jesus taught. Repetition indicates emphasis, and using the word "follow" twice in quick succession serves to emphasize that discipleship is part of the gospel.

Following Jesus is an active process; it involves *doing* what he says, not just hearing it. We need to rekindle this idea among God's people today, and that's why we've emphasized discipleship in our definition. I (Ben) will never forget the moment this really hit home for me. I was sitting in a seminary class on the Book of Revelation. My professor, Dr. Hoehner, took us verse-by-verse through the book of Revelation *in Greek*. It was "all Greek to me," but I loved it! The unforgettable moment happened when we read Revelation 20:12: "And the dead were judged by what was written in the books, according to what they had done." We went on to read the next verse, which repeats the same concept: "They were judged, each of them according to what they had done" (20:13).

Dr. Hoehner raised his face from the page, looked at us over his wiry glasses, and asked, "How were they judged?" One of my classmates piped up and said, "According to what they had done." There was a long silence after that. Dr. Hoenher was a great teacher, and he simply said after the silence, "You should think about that." I did think about it, and you should, too. There's no salvation apart from a life characterized by obedience.

111

One Gospel, Different Language

Our gospel definition isn't *the only answer*, but just one example to get you started with your own definition. As we work with pastors and ministry leaders through The Bonhoeffer Project, we start by helping them define the gospel, using our gospel definition as an example. Bonhoeffer participants analyze the gospel they have been preaching, study the gospel Jesus preached in the Bible, and then rebuild the gospel they preach to align with Jesus' gospel—one that includes discipleship. We focus on defining the gospel before we get to the mechanics of how to make disciples because *the gospel you preach determines the disciples you make*.

In this rebuilding process, we use the one hundred-word definition as a foundation for others. Our cohort participants don't just copy it, though; their gospel definition is built around the structure of 1 Corinthians 15:3-4. We encourage them to include the four declarative statements of the gospel proper and Jesus' three imperative responses. They often use other biblical language that's specific to their ministry context and culture.

There is one gospel but different biblical language to express it. When we considered the importance of God's kingdom for the gospel in Part 2, we saw that while Jesus primarily used kingdom-coming language, the apostles predominately used creation-restoration language. Even within the Bible, authors use different language, but it's the same gospel message.

Tim Keller describes the importance of crafting a contextualized definition of the gospel in his article, "The Gospel In All Its Forms":

> Today there are many who doubt that there is just one gospel.
> That gives them the warrant to ignore the gospel of atonement and
> justification. There are others who don't like to admit that there are
> different forms to that one gospel. That smacks too much of 'contextualization,' a term they dislike. They cling to a single presentation
> that is often one-dimensional. Neither of these approaches is as true to
> the biblical material, nor as effective in actual ministry as that which
> understands that the Bible presents one gospel in several forms.[8]

Essentially, Keller is saying with us that there is one gospel with several biblical ways to express it.

Disciple Making vs. Spiritual Parenting

We see a similar divergence of language with discipleship, too. Jesus mostly used the language of *disciple making*, but the apostles often used the language of *spiritual parenting*. Paul, for example, calls his young disciple, Timothy, his "true child in the faith" (1 Tim. 1:2).[9] The Apostle John also uses parenting language instead of direct discipleship language by using terms like "fathers," "young men," and "children" (1 John 2:11-14). Whether defining the gospel or defining discipleship, biblical writers employ a certain measure of latitude with regard to language, and so can we.

As you begin to embrace different language but use the same gospel, it might feel squirrely. You may be tempted to think that different language equals different gospels, but resist the temptation. It's critical to always keep coming back to the strong framework of 1 Corinthians 15:3-4 and the essential elements of the gospel in Mark 1 and 8. Keep coming back to the gospel Jesus preached, to which he called his disciples. Although it might be said of us or our definitions, there's nothing squirrely about Christ or unclear about his gospel. We should use it as the plumb line by which we measure the gospel we believe and preach.

Concluding Definition Thoughts

As we conclude this chapter on defining the gospel, we have three thoughts. First, our gospel definition reminds us that when you listen to the way people talk about being a disciple, many of them—even prominent leaders in disciple-making movements—make it sound like you can be a Christian and not be a disciple. But a Christian and a disciple aren't two different things; they're one and the same. At this point in this book, another underlying assumption clearly rises to the surface, and this is our third one: you cannot be a Christian and not be a disciple. To state it positively, *all Christians are disciples*. As soon as we define the discipleship gospel in clear terms (like we have done above), this becomes evident.

We're convinced that the type of thinking that says *you can be a Christian and not be a disciple* is nothing more than a clever cover for disobedience. It enables people to say that they believe in Jesus without being held accountable to actually obeying Jesus. Jesus didn't know of such a gap. He didn't give us room to lag or sag into disobedience. In their book, *The Trellis and the Vine*, Colin Marshall and Tony Payne write, "*All* Christians should be trained to be disciple-making disciples" (emphasis ours).[10] This truth is one of the reasons we have titled this book "the discipleship gospel"—because faith in the gospel leads to a life of discipleship. As such, we must stop thinking that a disciple is only someone who is a "serious Christian." Christians are disciples; otherwise, they're not Christians.

A second concluding thought on defining the gospel is to beware as you dare to define the gospel: *you will* encounter opposition as soon as you do. Unfortunately, there is a demented stream of thought that floats in and out of Christian circles today which resists any type of gospel definition. Many people, we've found, think that stating the gospel succinctly is dangerous. Although we've tried to understand this type of resistance, we don't. We've found that those who resist a gospel definition are actually part of the gospel problem, not the solution. There are some heavy hitters in the Christian world, though, who resist a gospel definition, so we don't say this lightly. No matter how scholarly these people might sound or how famous they are, Christians need to know what the gospel is. And they won't know that unless we who have a clear understanding help them define it!

Finally, as we wrap up this chapter, it's noteworthy that most books about the gospel—surprisingly—don't really offer a clear definition of the gospel. If they do, they define it in such a way that does not practically equip pastors in pulpits or people in pews. It's either way too long to wrap our minds around, so short that it's unhelpful, or it's missing one or more of the essential elements of Jesus' gospel. As such, many books about the gospel are, for all practical purposes, impractical.

We hope this book ruffles some feathers—in a good way, to be sure—but we also want it to be practical and helpful. We want to define the gospel in a way that equips the church—everyone from the pulpit to the pews and beyond—with a full understanding of Jesus' gospel, one that empowers disciples to make disciples. Now that we have succinctly defined the discipleship gospel in narrative form, let's consider how the gospel empowers discipleship in our lives and the life of the church.

10

DISCIPLESHIP BEGINS IN THE PULPIT

"It all started by Jesus calling a few men to follow him.
This revealed immediately the direction his evangelistic
strategy would take. His concern was not with programs
to reach the multitudes, but with men whom the
multitudes would follow."

—ROBERT COLEMAN

If you're not a pastor, you still need to read this chapter. As you start read-ing, it might seem like it's for pastors only, but it's not. Even though much of this chapter is *about* pastors, it's written *for all Christians* because we're all are called to be disciple-making leaders in the church—whether we know it or not.

If you're not a pastor, then, how should you use this chapter? First, if your pastor is not a disciple-making leader and they're not intentionally dis-cipling a few people at a time, please don't shove this book in their face and say, "You need to read this!" That's about as effective as when a husband or wife jabs their spouse in the ribs at a marriage conference to reinforce a point. Instead, begin praying—pray that what we describe in this chapter would become true of your pastor. All too often, we discount the importance and effectiveness of prayer, so use this chapter to pray for your pastor that they might become a dynamic, disciple-making leader.

More than this, non-pastors will be able to apply almost all the content of this chapter to their own life with the exception of the part about *preaching every Sunday*. We've chosen to direct our words specifically to pastors here because if anyone needs to *know* and *do* these things in the church, it's pastors. Pastors have authority from God to influence their church. But when you read in this chapter about pastors intentionally discipling a few people at a time, you need to be doing that, too. If you believe in the gospel, you're called to be a disciple-making leader.

Start With the Gospel

So as we think about how to impact an entire church, we must first ask the question, *What does it look like to be a disciple-making church?* To start, a disciple-making church has a clear definition of the discipleship gospel, as we have been saying. If this isn't the starting point, the church is doomed for failure right from the start. A gospel that calls people to be disciples and make disciples is the only thing that continues to empower disciple making in the church; it's the only sustainable fuel for disciple making in the church. If you try to keep it running on anything else—hype, a pastor's charisma, a great curriculum, etc.—it will run out of gas—guaranteed. Remember that the gospel you preach determines the disciples you make.

A clear declaration of the discipleship gospel at the heart of the church is critical for all disciple making in the church. Not only does it help correct the fatal error of allowing discipleship to be considered as optional, it also breeds clarity among the congregation about what the gospel is. A clear, succinct, written declaration also enables viral reproducibility. In other words, it can be published and propagated. For example, at Cypress (Ben's church), we printed our gospel definition on our website, printed it on 3x5 cards for distribution in our congregation, included it in our new member's guide, and made it part of our main discipleship tool. Disciple making in the church begins with having and making known a specific gospel definition.

The Pastor and the Pulpit

If our churches are going to make disciples, we need to be thoroughly saturated with the gospel. Ideally, discipleship in the local church begins in the pulpit with a pastor who is committed to preaching the discipleship gospel and seeing their congregation transformed into a disciple-making force for the advancing of God's kingdom.

If the pastor isn't willing to preach the discipleship gospel, it's going to be a hard row to hoe. As Dallas Willard once said to me (Bill), "It's tough to plow around the pulpit."[1] That is, if the pastor isn't preaching the discipleship gospel from the pulpit, then the congregation is not hearing about:

- God's kingdom,
- Jesus being the Christ,
- His death and resurrection,
- His call for people to repent, believe, and follow him, and
- How all these relate to each other as essential elements of the gospel

When a congregation isn't regularly hearing the whole gospel, gospel confusion ensues. This also severely disables discipleship in the church as a whole. As Greg Ogden says, "Preaching at its best calls people to become disciples."[2]

Discipleship in the local church begins with pastors who are unafraid to preach the discipleship gospel; it's a great joy to do this, but it's not for the faint of heart. Jesus promised that the gates of hell will not overcome the church (Matt. 16:18), but that's not a promise hell won't vehemently attack the church back—only that it won't overcome its progress! If there are focal points for the full-frontal attacks of hell upon the church, one of them is the pulpit and the person in it. If the devil can take a pastor down in any way, you better believe he'll do it!

If only one person in the church has crystal clarity on the gospel, considers the gospel of first importance, and believes that the gospel is the mighty power of God for the salvation of everyone who believes, they need to be that church's pastor. If a pastor doesn't want these things to be true of them, they should step down from their position. If our churches are going to make disciples, we need discipleship-gospel preachers.

Preaching Through a Specific Gospel

One of the best ways for pastors to begin teaching their congregation the gospel is by preaching through one of the four New Testament Gospels. As we observed above, Matthew, Mark, Luke, and John are called "Gospels" because they were written to reveal the fullness of the gospel. As such, they give the church the greatest insights into the beauty of Jesus and his life on earth. They also show the power of his message and the amazing patterns of his disciple-making methods (1 Pet. 2:21).

When we say, "preach through one of the Gospels," we actually mean for your church to read through one of the Gospels verse by verse as a congregation, starting from the pulpit. Don't pick and choose this or that passage or avoid "the hard sayings" of Jesus. Read every verse and preach through all of it. As the pastor, allow Jesus to challenge you during your preparation and your preaching (especially surrendering to him your preconceived ideas about the gospel and discipleship).

Early in our friendship, Bill encouraged me (Ben) to preach through one of the New Testament Gospels, so I did. As a result, I learned firsthand that good things happen in a church when a pastor preaches through a Gospel with their congregation. I chose Mark's Gospel, and it just so happened that I did this while I was in one of the first cohorts of The Bonhoeffer Project. To do these two activities in tandem proved to be transformational—both for our congregation and for me. I began my preparation for preaching through Mark's Gospel by reading one chapter each week on my own and doing an exposition of that chapter from the pulpit on Sunday morning. We did this for sixteen weeks (one week per chapter). Then, our congregation gathered midweek in sermon-based small groups to dig even deeper into the same passage.

As we read and studied Mark's gospel together, Jesus spoke, and we listened. When he served the poor, we encouraged each other to do the same. When he challenged his original twelve disciples, we allowed him to challenge us, too. We paid much closer attention and made it a point to put his teachings into practice. In doing this together, our church began seeing the essential elements of Jesus' gospel revealed in the pages of Scripture. We saw his patterns for disciple making laid out for us. While this was going on, I was experiencing a gospel and discipleship renewal with Bill and the Bonhoeffer cohort I had joined.[3]

By the time our congregation had completed Mark's Gospel and I had graduated from The Bonhoeffer Project, our church had done a lot of deep discipleship work, which included:

- Defining the gospel
- Defining a "disciple"
- Creating a comprehensive discipleship strategy that was unique to our church and purposed every ministry for discipleship
- Adding an intentional disciple-making ministry
- Forming our own church's discipleship tool that was grounded in Mark's Gospel and included our definitions and strategy

These things were tangible items that we had put on paper. There were other things too, though, that emerged—intangible things. Our congregation began speaking the gospel to one another, for example, and talking about discipleship more often. This created a common language and an expectation for disciple making in our congregation. Our common language began forming a culture of discipleship among us. Now, three years later, our church's discipleship culture is still forming, but the genesis of this transition stemmed from one core activity: preaching through one of the New Testament Gospels from the pulpit. We highly recommend this, and Mark's Gospel can be a great place to start (because it's short and punchy), even though the other Gospels can work well, too.

Now, if you're not a pastor, how do you apply this? You may want to consider meeting with two or three others in your congregation or ministry context to read through a Gospel together. As you do, pay particular attention to Jesus' gospel message and also to his disciple-making methods. Be sure not to allow this to become *just another Bible study*. Studying the Bible is good—very good—but if you don't put Jesus' teaching into practice, your efforts will lose their power. On this point, Jesus lays down a "use it or lose it" principle with respect to his teaching on more than one occasion (Mark 4:25). We'll discuss the specifics, dynamics, and benefits of forming a discipleship group of three or four with greater detail in the next chapter.

A Disciple-Making Pastor

One of the most powerful ways to start a disciple-making movement in a church is for the pastor to begin preaching the discipleship gospel from the pulpit, calling people to be disciples who make disciples as a natural part of responding to the gospel. When you combine this with a pastor who is also personally making disciples of church members and others in the community, it's exponentially more effective in our experience. In fact, we'd go so far as to say that this is a recipe for catalytic change toward disciple making in a church. A pastor can preach all they want about discipleship, but until they actually start making disciples, their words will "fall to the ground" (1 Sam. 3:19). In other words, pastors need to practice what they preach.

Some pastors have convinced themselves that making disciples is preaching sermons, shepherding people through births, weddings, and funerals, and keeping all the programs of the church running. This is different, though, than what we see Jesus doing in the Gospels. Jesus preached and ministered to the crowds, but he also intentionally discipled a few by spending significant time with them. In fact, the longer Jesus ministered, the less time he spent with the crowds, and the more time he spent discipling a few.

As men who have firsthand experience leading a church, we know how busy and distracted a pastor can be. But we're convinced that there's no excuse to not make disciples, *especially* if you're the pastor. If any one person is to obey the Great Commission in the church, it must be the pastor. If you as the pastor aren't making time to make disciples, you can't expect anyone else in the church to do it.

One reason, however, so many pastors aren't makings disciples in their church is that they've never been discipled. You can't be an expert in what you haven't experienced. As humbling as it may be to realize this (and maybe even embarrassing), it's a common story. Pastors may have even attended Bible college, taken seminary courses, learned to preach sermons and manage church programs, but none of these educational experiences can substitute for someone intentionally investing themselves into your life and strengthening you through encouragement to follow Jesus. A surprising number of pastors have never experienced this.

In my (Bill's) book, *The Disciple-Making Pastor*, I wrote about the vital importance of disciple-making pastors:

> Not much will change until we raise the issue and create controversy, until the American church is challenged to take the Great Commission seriously, until pastors are willing to start reproducing themselves through others, to prepare people to be self-feeding Christians, until congregations allow pastors to spend most of their time on teaching and training the spiritually well minority, rather than servicing the whims and desires of the unmotivated and disobedient majority, until pastors can be unleashed from evangelical "busy work." It must be done, we can't allow this to continue; there must be a change.[4]

I wrote these words nearly thirty years ago, and for the longest time, I didn't see much change. Over the last few years, though, things have begun to change as pastors have started adopting the "discipleship-first" value and more and more people in the pews are showing themselves to be "fourth soil" believers (see Mark 4:1-20).

When we talk to pastors from around the country who are preaching the discipleship gospel with passion and who intentionally make disciples, many of them agree that there was a moment when everything changed for them. They talk about coming to a point where they stopped making excuses and determined to start making disciples. Do you want to know what changed them? It was the moment they realized that *not making disciples* was the same thing as *sinning*. They became convinced that not fulfilling the Great Commission was disobedience. When they got to that point and repented of not making disciples, everything changed.

Whether you're in the pulpit or sitting in the pew on Sunday morning, you need to know that disciple making in the church ideally begins with the person in the pulpit. If a pastor is committed to defining the discipleship gospel and preaching it faithfully Sunday after Sunday, it can spark a disciple-making fire in their church. If you're not a pastor, pray for a discipleship breakthrough in your congregation—that your pastor will come to know and gain the courage to preach the discipleship gospel, as well  as personally make disciples—that will be the first major breakthrough. If you pray for the pastor and over time they don't become a disciple maker, pray that the Lord will remove them.

Some pastors are doing this, yet they are not witnessing a revival of discipleship in their congregation. Why not? One reason for this is that the fire of discipleship must jump from the pulpit into the pews. The people in the pews need to start making disciples! When that happens, look out, because you'll have a disciple-making movement ready to break out, which is exactly what we investigate in the next chapter.

11

FROM THE PULPIT TO THE PEW

"If this world is going to be reached [with the gospel],
I am convinced it must be done by men and women of
average talent."

—D.L. MOODY

In our experience, the chances of a discipleship revolution breaking out is extremely low in a church in which the pastor is not preaching the discipleship gospel and personally making disciples. It's possible (nothing is impossible with God), but in our experience, it's nearly impossible if the pastor isn't doing it, and it's very unlikely that a majority of the congregation ever will either. As the old saying goes, "A mist in the pulpit is a fog in the pews."

There may be a small contingent of disciple makers in the pews even when the pastor in the pulpit isn't a disciple maker, but it's hard to be a disciple-making leader in a non-disciple-making church. If you're among such a small group, we beg you to not grow weary in disciple making and to not give up. Your faithfulness in making disciples and the fruit of your labor of love—which is the changed lives of your disciples—just may cause others in the church, including the pastor, to sit up and take notice.

Whether you're leading from the pulpit or from the pew, if you try to start a disciple-making movement in your church, begin by discipling only "fourth soilers." If you disciple enough fourth soilers, and they begin to multiply—as fourth soilers often do—you can reach the tipping point of creating a disciple-making movement with a local congregation.

Discipling Only "Fourth Soilers"

Your decision of whom you select to disciple is critical, so you must begin by discipling people in the church who will become the disciple-making leaders of the church. They might not be those type of leaders yet, but they should be fourth-soil kind of people already. We call these people fourth soilers because they are like the fourth-soil people Jesus describes in his parable of the sower in Mark 4. These are people who hear God's Word, put it into practice, and multiply thirty, sixty, and one hundred times.

Fourth soilers are not necessarily "the best and the brightest" or even the people to whom you naturally gravitate. It's often only through prayer and time that you discover the two or three fourth soilers to whom God wants you to devote yourself for the next months of your life. Jesus prayed all night before he selected his twelve disciples, and he chose twelve extremely different men. Each one was, apparently, very ordinary (Acts 4:13). Jesus' selection of his disciples is the only time on record that he prayed all night about something.

Pray that God will direct you to fourth soilers. Some might be older, while others may be younger; some may have similar interests to yours, while others may be nothing like you. Just as God selected David to be king of Israel based on his heart and not by outward appearance, we encourage you to also choose people to disciple based on the prayerful discernment of the heart (1 Sam. 16:7). Pray for people who love Jesus, obey Jesus, and actually want to be discipled. After you've prayed and have some direction, invite these people to your discipleship group. If they say "yes" and a couple of others do, too, you're on your way to being a disciple-making leader. Don't underestimate the importance of your choice of disciples. If you don't disciple fourth soilers or people who become fourth soilers, don't expect to create a disciple-making movement because only fourth soilers multiply—and a disciple-making movement demands multiplication.

Begin making disciples with people like Dave, who is a fourth soiler at my (Ben's) church. When I started making disciples with just a few guys,

Dave was one of them. Dave, who is now an older man, had been discipled when he was a new disciple. This early discipleship experience deeply impacted Dave. He gives thanks for it all the time. When I began leading discipleship groups at Cypress, Dave joined me in leading his own groups, and we grew in disciple making together.

After several years of leading discipleship groups, God gave Dave a passion for discipling younger men in our congregation, not just other men in general. He meets with three or four young men at a time over months to study Scripture, pray, and share lessons he's learned about being a Christian man and husband with them. Dave's disciple making has a strong Titus 2 *older man-younger man* feel to it. Just as Dave had been discipled as a young man, now as an older man, he is discipling young men. When you begin making disciples, start with fourth soilers like Dave.

So How Do We Do This?

Once you've prayerfully gathered two or three fourth soilers, what's next? A common disciple-making question that we need to answer is the most basic question of all: *how do you make disciples?* This question is followed by a flurry of other, very practical questions:

- When do you meet?
- Where do you disciple people?
- What exactly do you do with those you're discipling?
- How long do you invest in them?
- What curriculum do you use, if any?

We believe you can find the answer to all of these questions by studying how Jesus made disciples in the Gospels. Study what he said *and* what he did. Then, put his example into practice and do it. Be prepared to fail as you implement what you learn, but learn from your "failures" and grow as you gain experience. One thing you *must not do* is give up. As author Eugene Peterson calls it, discipleship is "a long obedience in the same direction."[1]

Don't *ever* force or guilt someone into discipleship. Nothing will cause disciple making to fail faster in a church than some kind of coercion. Before they get started, a leader can shoot their disciple-making efforts in the foot by guilting people into making disciples. Disciple making is a "get to," not a "have to," kind of thing. People need to make disciples out of joyful, loving obedience to Jesus, not because someone has played some sort of manipulative mind game on them. While Jesus requires it of people, we cannot come in as "the enforcers." If you're working on creating a disciple-making movement in your church, you don't want people in discipleship groups who don't really want to be there. Don't force people to make disciples. Trust us on this one—we've learned the hard way. Now, let's consider several other aspects of how Jesus made disciples.

Groups of Three or Four

Jesus chose twelve men out of the great crowd to disciple. The Twelve get much of his attention, as they should because they're important. It's surprising how little focus is given to "the Three," though. Jesus chose the Twelve, but he also selected the inner three: Peter, James, and John. He set them apart on a number of occasions during his ministry and spent more time with them. In fact, the Three were the only ones with Jesus during some of his greatest highs and lows.

Jesus seems to have had his eye on them from the beginning because the Three were among the first people Jesus called to follow him (Mark 1:16-20). They were the only disciples to see Jesus raise a dead girl back to life, to witness Jesus' glorious transfiguration, to hear his end-time prophecies on the Mount of Olives, and to be near him as he prayed "not my will but your will" in Gethsemane (Mark 5:37; 9:2; 13:3; 14:33). Also, let's not forget that Peter, who was one of the Three, was the first disciple to confess that Jesus was the Christ.

Jesus discipled the Twelve, but he also set apart the Three for discipleship purposes. This isn't inconsequential; the Three should be instructive to us as we consider how to make disciples.

The dynamics of discipleship groups of three or four are unique among all the discipleship environments of the church. Jesus ministered to the crowds (Mark 3:7), the Seventy-Two (Luke 10:1), the Twelve (Matt. 10:1), the Three (Mark 3:37), and he spent time with people one-on-one (John 4:10). All these "discipleship environments" represented in Jesus' ministry are often reflected by various ministries in the church. Yet, of all the various sized ministries of a church, there is an intimacy, a level of shared experience, and accountability in groups of three or four that neither one-on-one relationships nor larger groups enjoy in quite the same way. When Cypress (Ben's church) implemented discipleship groups, we started with groups of three or four. We've discovered it to be the most transformative size.

Our friend Greg Ogden highlights the strengths of these "micro groups," as he calls them in his book, *Transforming Discipleship: Making Disciples a Few at a Time*. In it, he writes: "We could close the discipleship gap if we adopted Jesus' approach. By investing in a few [...] Jesus was able to encourage and guide his disciples to internalize his message and mission."[2] In our work with The Bonhoeffer Project, we consistently see God use discipleship groups of three and four to bring about enduring transformation in people's lives and to create disciple-making movements in churches.

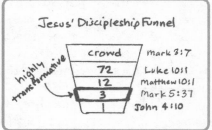

This shouldn't surprise us. As Pastor Craig Etheredge says in *Invest in a Few*, "This was Jesus' strategy. It was quite simple—every disciple makes disciples. Every Christ follower invests in a few."[3] In light of how Jesus discipled the Three, it's surprising that we don't see more discipleship groups of this size gathering in our churches and serving together in the community. We're not suggesting that this is the only way to make disciples; it's not because every ministry of the local church has a discipleship purpose (or at least it should). But since Jesus himself set apart three disciples, it might be something we should at least consider.

Disciple Others Through the Gospels

The Gospels were written for the purpose of discipleship—so that we could learn what the gospel is, what it means to be a disciple, and how to make disciples. For example, Luke states that his purpose in writing his account of Jesus' life was so we might have "certainty concerning the things [we] have been taught" about Jesus (Luke 1:4). All four Gospels were written with a similar purpose—to disciple us into believing in and living out the gospel. The result is that we are equipped to follow Jesus.[4]

Our (Ben's) church has designed a simple tool to guide our discipleship groups through Mark's Gospel. We originally named it *Follow*, but since then we've published it as *The Discipleship Gospel Workbook: Multiply Disciples with the Gospel of Mark* to make it more broadly available as curriculum for discipleship groups.[5] When our church's discipleship groups of three and four meet, we use this curriculum as we read every verse of Mark's Gospel, one chapter at a time. This tool helps us apply what we're learning, putting into practice what Jesus either *taught* his disciples or *did* with his disciples.

A short time ago, I was forming a discipleship group. Now, I had asked Bob (the older man I wrote about earlier, who was a new convert). I also had Garrett, a twenty-five-year old surfer, and the Lord had laid it on my heart to pray for one more man. A few weeks later, a man named Randy called me at church. Randy and I had met several years before, but we hadn't seen each other in some time. He called to see if we could get together to catch up and talk about a few things (unrelated to discipleship). We got together a couple of days later.

While Randy and I met over coffee, out of the blue he said, "This is going to sound strange, but I think Jesus is calling me to learn how to follow him." As soon as he said this, alarms went off in my head, and I thought, *Is this the guy I've been praying for?* We  talked about discipleship, and he was eager to learn more. I smiled, ran to my truck, pulled out the workbook, ran back to Randy, and showed him the title. When he read the word "Follow" on the front cover (it's name at the time), he laughed—hard. He laughed because he had been praying for an opportunity to learn about *following* Jesus. I didn't know it at the time, but my actions that day were part of an answer to his prayers. The Lord opened up the opportunity for him to learn more about following Jesus, and he answered my prayer for one more guy. That's the power of God to bring together a group for discipleship.

Putting Jesus' Teaching Into Practice

Here's a practical example of *putting Jesus' teaching into practice* using *The Discipleship Gospel Workbook*; it comes from how our discipleship groups study Mark 5. In this chapter of the Gospel, Jesus takes his disciples to "the other side."[6] For Jesus' Jewish disciples—who did everything they could to stay ritually "clean," according to the Old Testament Law—"the other side" was dripping with "uncleanness;" it was unclean Gentile territory with unclean Gentile men, unclean spirits, unclean tombs, and unclean pigs. It just didn't get more unclean than that! It was the last place the disciples would've normally wanted to go, but they went because they were following Jesus.

After reading about "the other side" in Mark 5, we prompt our discipleship groups to talk about where "the other side" of our city is. Wherever we decide it is, we go there to serve others in Jesus' name. It's often Soledad Street in Salinas, California. Soledad Street is well known for drugs, gangs, homelessness, and prostitution. After "the other side" experience, our discipleship groups have learned a critical lesson: discipleship isn't just about reading Jesus' words and actions, it's also about putting them into practice (Jam. 1:22). By taking action, we learn to obey. The most transformative discipleship experiences are not knowledge-based, but obedience-based.

Mark's Gospel is sixteen chapters long, which means our discipleship groups meet for at least sixteen weeks or four months. Four months, though, ends up being more like six months once you've coordinated three or four peoples' schedules. We meet for at least an hour and half, often using the first twenty minutes to ask each other one of our four discipleship questions, fifty minutes to study a chapter of Mark's Gospel, and twenty minutes to plan our "putting it into practice project" before our next training.

Boot Camp-Like Training

We designed *The Discipleship Gospel Workbook* to be a boot camp-like experience that helps disciples learn the basics of following Jesus, or "the elementary doctrine of Christ," as the writer of Hebrews calls them (Heb. 6:1). As such, we understand that going through Mark's Gospel like this is a training experience like what the Apostle Paul writes about three times in just three verses in his first letter to his young protégé Timothy. He writes:

> If you put these things before the brothers, you will be a good servant of Christ Jesus, being *trained in the words of faith and of the good doctrine that you have followed.* Have nothing to do with irreverent, silly myths. Rather *train yourself for godliness;* for while bodily *training* is of some value, godliness is of value in every way, as it holds promise for the present life and also for the life to come.
>
> —1 Timothy 4:6-8
> (*emphasis ours*)

As a church, we view this initial discipleship experience as a first step in fulfilling our calling to "equip the saints for the work of the ministry" (Eph. 4:12).

One "elementary doctrine" that Mark's Gospel trains us in is the gospel itself. This being the case, our workbook curriculum is evangelistic. It teaches people what the gospel is and calls them to believe in it—to repent, believe, and follow Jesus. As such, we've used it with unbelievers, new believers, and undiscipled believers as a foundational experience for following Jesus. We investigate other evangelistic aspects of discipleship in greater detail in the next chapter of this book.

Every Ministry Has Discipleship Purpose

Every ministry of a local church has a critical discipleship purpose. This is important to state, especially in light of our emphasis on discipleship groups of three and four. While a church might make discipleship groups of three and four the heart of their discipleship strategy, it doesn't mean that the other ministries of the church are somehow less important or not included as "discipleship." When all ministries, including discipleship groups, are connected and purposed *for discipleship*, the discipleship dynamics in the church multiply exponentially.

Sunday services, small groups, children's ministry, youth ministry, young adult's ministry, men's ministry, women's ministry, senior's ministry, serving opportunities, and community outreach—all these ministries advance a church's disciple-making efforts. The trick is learning how they all fit together and defining their specific discipleship purpose. Stating the discipleship purpose of a specific ministry isn't easy, but it's worth it.

Developing a written statement identifying the purpose for each ministry and how each relates to making disciples is critical if you're going to crack the discipleship code in your church. It's "the last ten percent" that is often left undone. It involves digging into Scripture and creating purpose statements for each ministry that clearly connect to biblical mandates. This language will shape the discipleship culture of your congregation, so it's important to make the purpose statements precise. It's also critical that your church has a specific disciple-making ministry when possible. Lastly, we urge you to define the discipleship purpose of each ministry in your church so that all your members can grow to understand how everything your church does seeks to fulfill Christ's Great Commission (Matt. 28:18-20).

12

DISCIPLESHIP IS EVANGELISM

"Evangelism that focuses on decisions short circuits and—
yes, the word is appropriate—aborts the design of the
gospel, while evangelism that aims at disciples slows down
to offer the full gospel of Jesus and the apostles."

—Scot McKnight

One of the greatest weaknesses in local churches today is that we lead people to Christ and then, basically, abandon them. It's "hit and run" evangelism. In our experience, if members of American congregations evangelize at all, which is rare, the goal is to get their victim to repeat the sinner's prayer. If they say the prayer, the Christian claims victory by announcing that person to be "a new believer." Then, they invite them to church and hope they come.

If they do come to church (which is highly unlikely), we give them a Bible, introduce them to a couple of people, and label them as part of a "follow-up" task. This makes us feel like we've fulfilled our duty. While "hit and run" evangelism should be a crime, we've grown quite comfortable with it in the church today.

Hit and run evangelism, with its limited follow up, falls far short of discipling someone "until Christ is formed in [them]," as Paul writes (Gal. 4:19). The problem is that only a handful of churches in every community (if that) have a clear and comprehensive plan for intentionally discipling people until they are established in the faith and fully integrated into the community of the church. If you don't have a plan, you don't intend to do it. While this might sound like an overstatement, it's not. We interact with hundreds of pastors every year through The Bonhoeffer Project, and a precious few have such a plan, which is why they're talking to us in the first place. By the way, this includes pastors of large, "successful," and growing churches. So just because your church is growing with numerical growth doesn't necessarily mean that you're making disciples.

The root of this problem is that Christians have separated conversion from discipleship. Today, we've come to think of these as two different and unrelated things, rather than two intermingled phases of one new life. When the church divorces conversion and discipleship, the focus of the church shifts almost exclusively to conversion, or evangelism, which becomes first priority and, in turn, makes discipleship a secondary issue—essentially, a non-essential part of our lives as Christians. It's rare to find a church that has a comprehensive discipleship strategy (also known as a plan) and a fully equipped team to disciple new followers of Jesus. In this chapter, we'll address some of these skewed ways of thinking and practices, and we hope to convince you that discipleship actually *is evangelism.*

Evangelizing the Church

Before we send church members to evangelize the world, we first need to thoroughly evangelize our church members. You might think, *Why do we need to evangelize believers? They already believe!* We don't usually think about evangelizing the church. Instead, we've come to understand evangelism as being for unbelievers and discipleship as being for believers (if we think that discipleship is for anyone at all). But this is a false and dangerous separation because the Bible doesn't divide evangelism from discipleship. That is, the gospel isn't only for the purpose of converting unbelievers; the gospel is the church's glorious story, and we need to continually rehearse it to one another and with one another.

How does this work? We thoroughly "evangelize" church members by *discipling* every member in the gospel and constantly *reminding* them of the gospel. When we do this, the gospel defines the entire life of a Christian. It's not something we believed in at some point in the past with no need for it anymore. As Paul equivocally declares, the gospel is "of first importance" in the church (1 Cor. 15:3).

Our faith in the gospel is what empowers us to follow Jesus daily. As we learned earlier, following Jesus is living a new life defined by dying to ourselves every day and living in the power of Christ's resurrection. This requires that we, the church, continually rehearse the glorious, life-defining story of the gospel with one another. Such rehearsal keeps us crystal clear on what the gospel is. It equips us to encourage one another with the gospel, and it also prepares us to proclaim it to others who are lost and without Christ in the world.

When you have a way of intentionally discipling people in the "elementary doctrine of Christ" (as we considered in the previous chapter), it's a game changer. This elementary doctrine must include the gospel. It's surprising how many discipleship curricula don't train people on the gospel and how to articulate it fully yet succinctly—indicators that even the disciple-making leaders who are writing these discipleship curricula have separated evangelism from discipleship. We fully believe (and have experienced) that the best way to discover the truth of the gospel is in the context of intentional, discipling relationships.

Discipleship
=
Evangelism

Whatever discipleship curriculum you use, be sure it trains people with the gospel and how to articulate it. And make sure that it actually calls people to repent and believe in the gospel and to begin following Jesus. A discipleship curriculum that includes these gospel aspects is an evangelistic tool that also empowers believers to rehearse the gospel with one another. It can be used to disciple interested unbelievers, eager new believers, and fourth soil believers to become disciple-making catalysts of the church. It also helps us to see that discipleship becomes evangelism.

Jesus' Primary Method of Evangelism

Let's unpack the statement "discipleship becomes evangelism" by looking at the life of Christ. Of all the methods of evangelism that Jesus demonstrated in the Gospels—and there were many—the one highlighted above all the others is discipleship. Jesus preached the gospel to great crowds, and he shared it with people one on one. But the Gospel writers keep bringing us back to the fact that Jesus discipled a few good men in what the gospel was and how they were to live it out. For Jesus, discipleship was how he evangelized both the men in whom he invested and the people they reached as a result. We suggest that the Gospel writers were clear that discipleship was Jesus' most effective method of evangelism. In other words, the gospel seemed to "stick" best with those whom Jesus discipled most.

Reading the Gospels gives us the distinct sense that Jesus' discipleship of the Twelve was an experience of "one step forward, two steps back." Just as it looks like the disciples are getting it, they do something that shows they don't (what was true of them at that time is also true of us now). Jesus walked a long way with them before the gospel was truly formed in them; it took them a long time to really know what the gospel was and even longer to begin denying themselves, taking up their cross daily, and follow Jesus in the power of his resurrection.

When we think about it like this, we start to realize that the gospel wasn't fully formed in the disciples' hearts until sometime after Jesus' resurrection. No matter when you pinpoint the moment the disciples actually "got it," our aim here is to show that discipleship among the Twelve was evangelism for Jesus—and it took time.

This is what Scot McKnight refers to (at the beginning of this chapter) when he writes of evangelism that "slows down to offer the full gospel of Jesus and the apostles."[1] It's also what pastor and author (*The Message*) Eugene Peterson speaks of when he says that "forming people in Christ is a slow work, so it can't be hurried; it is an urgent work, so it can't be delayed."[2] The most transformative environment for maturing people into Christlikeness happens when we allow people the time they need to come into a full understanding of the gospel in the context of committed discipleship relationships. This was true in Jesus' ministry, and it is no different in the local church today. It's the opposite of "hit and run" evangelism.

I (Ben) remember talking with one of our ministry leaders a few years ago about multiplying disciples within our congregation. We had just begun intentionally making disciples in groups of three and four, and he asked, "Who are we going to start discipling?" I answered, "We're going to begin with our own members. Our goal is make sure every member has been given the opportunity to be discipled."

He thought for a moment and said, "What are you going to do after you've discipled all our church members? You won't have anyone left to disciple, will you?" I smiled and said, "I hope by that point our church members will be making disciples of people in our community and in other places." A puzzled look crossed his face. I realized that he had never thought about discipleship as a form of evangelism before. Discipleship, at its best, is evangelism.

No "Rocky Soilers" Allowed

We've talked about discipling all the "fourth soilers" in the church first—that is, if you want to create a disciple-making movement in your congregation. We want to add one more thing, though, for this to happen: in addition to discipling fourth soilers, the leaders of the church must also ensure no "rocky soilers" fall through the cracks and out of the church. "Rocky soilers" are the people Jesus described in Mark 4, who fell on the rocky soil in Jesus' Parable of the Sower. They are new followers of Jesus and very vulnerable.

Jesus describes these people as those who initially receive the seed of God's Word, the gospel, with joy, and everything looks good on the outside. They're following Jesus, and he even describes them as "enduring." He also says, though, that "they have no root in themselves." As soon as they face persecution or tribulation, "immediately they fall away" (Mark 4:17).

Fall away! What does that mean? It doesn't sound good. Let's take a closer look.

Two other passages—Galatians 5:4 and Hebrews 6:4-6—that also refer to those who "fall away" help us understand that falling away is bad. The Apostle Paul and the writer to the Hebrews wrote about people who were among the church but "fell away." We considered the situation with Paul in Galatia above, where Paul described these apostates by using the phrases "falling away from grace" and "severed from Christ" (Gal. 5:4). That's very serious language that communicates dramatic, even eternal, consequences.

In Hebrews 6:4-6, we also find a phrase referencing those who have "fallen away." The writer states:

> For it is impossible, in the case of those who have once been
> enlightened, who have tasted the heavenly gift, and have shared in
> the Holy Spirit, and have tasted the goodness of the word of God and

powers of the age to come, and then fallen away to restore them again to repentance, since they are crucifying once again the Son of God to their own harm and holding him up to contempt.

This passage reveals that in some situations, it's *impossible* to restore someone who has truly *fallen away* to repentance. Again, similar to Galatians 5:4, this is super-serious language.

The Leader's Responsibility

Obviously, both passages—Galatians 5:4 and Hebrews 6:4-6—are extreme cases. Whatever our interpretation of "falling away" is, at a bare minimum, we must at least recognize that new followers who are rocky soilers are at least vulnerable to this severe version of falling away. The description of "falling away" is the same language in Greek that's used in Mark 4, Galatians 5, and Hebrews 6. This means the leadership of a local church—those charged with shepherding people's souls—must not be content with someone receiving the gospel with joy and then letting them fend for themselves.

Instead, a church's shepherds need to take responsibility for new, vulnerable followers of Jesus. They need to ensure that new followers are discipled until Christ is formed in them (Gal. 4:19). This is a tall order. The leaders of our churches need to watch over new followers as they are taught "the elementary doctrine of Christ" (Heb. 6:1). And they need to exhort all followers of Jesus in their congregation to keep growing to maturity until they are fully equipped and engaged at some level in the kingdom-advancing gospel work of making disciples of all nations. A church's shepherds need to take responsibility for these things because they will be accountable for them (Acts 20:28).

How can a church's shepherds make sure these things happen? What does Jesus teach us to do with new, vulnerable followers? What do the apostles call a church's leaders to do with them? It's quite simple really—we are called to disciple them.

The Message Isn't the Method

As we think about evangelism, specifically about discipleship as evangelism, it's important to distinguish between the *message* of the gospel and a *method* of evangelism. This is particularly important with regard to defining the gospel for your congregation. There are many methods for evangelizing people—such as Steps to Peace with God, The Four Spiritual Laws, or Evangelism Explosion—but there is only one gospel message, the gospel Jesus preached.

The gospel message needs to be our primary source for understanding what the gospel is; it's our definition. Methods are expressions of the gospel, not a definition of it. In this sense, methods are one step removed from the gospel, and we should constantly be measuring our evangelistic methods against the gospel message itself. Evangelistic methods are supposed to communicate the fullness of the gospel message. Sometimes they do; sometimes they don't. Evangelistic methods don't always represent the fullness of the gospel, so be careful if you use them.

Knowing the difference between the message and the method impacts the way we make disciples. Before we train people in a specific evangelistic method, we should first disciple them in the gospel message. Doing this takes disciples back to the gospel itself, equipping them to determine whether particular methods flow from the original source or if they have been contaminated somehow. Teaching disciples the gospel message helps them stay away from "the different gospels" of which we spoke above.

gospel message ≠ evangelism method

These are the false gospels that the Apostle Paul says are double-cursed. We can't overstate the importance of not allowing an evangelistic method, as good as it may be, to become our definition of the gospel.

Mary Ann, a woman in my (Ben's) congregation, is on fire for Jesus. She was introduced to our gospel definition about a year ago and carefully worked through it and thoughtfully studied it. Afterwards, she came up to me on a Sunday morning with so much excitement.

"Pastor Ben, would you pray for a lady I met this week? I talked to her about Jesus and then got to share the gospel with her. I'm hoping she'll come to church to hear more." I did, and Mary Ann followed up with this woman to see if she would come to church with her.

The following Sunday, the woman came with Mary Ann to the worship service and loved it. The next Sunday, she, her husband, and their son came, too! When Mary Ann gained clarity on the gospel message, the Holy Spirit gave her great confidence to engage in evangelism. Mary Ann's story and what God did through her is a great illustration of how discipling people in the gospel leads to evangelism.

The Master Plan of Evangelism

In his classic work, *The Master Plan of Evangelism*, Dr. Robert Coleman conducts a biblical study of Jesus' method of making disciples. He highlights Jesus' process of selection, association, consecration, impartation, demonstration, delegation, supervision, and reproduction. It's a book all about discipleship—one of the best! But don't skip over the book's title: *The Master Plan of Evangelism*.

Why does this book, which is clearly about discipleship, have the word "evangelism" in the title? Is it false advertising? No, it's not. Dr. Coleman understands that discipleship *is evangelism*—Jesus' most effective method of evangelism. In fact, the title of his book actually began reviving our understanding of discipleship as evangelism.

13

CREATING A DISCIPLE-MAKING MOVEMENT

"The Christian ideal has not been tried and found
wanting. It has been found difficult; and left untried."

—G.K. CHESTERTON

You may have picked up on the progression of thought we're on here. It
starts with you (Chapter 10), then moves to your church (Chapters 11
and 12), and now we will describe how the discipleship gospel can create
disciple-making movements. Jesus' Great Commission couldn't have been
any clearer: he commanded the church to "make disciples of *all nations*"
(Matt. 28:18, emphasis ours). If you've been around the church for any length
of time, you've probably heard Matthew 28:18-20 referenced a thousand
times and heard those three verses taught using various angles. You might
have noticed how many people have mastered everything about the great
commission—except how to obey it. In our opinion, a church shouldn't be
allowed to refer to the Great Commission as "great" if they're ignoring it.

What we've found by talking to pastors and ministry leaders around the country through The Bonhoeffer Project is that church leaders are not refusing to make disciples, they're just unsure of *how* to make disciples—there's a huge difference between the two. Blatant disobedience is a black hole that leads to nowhere, but when leaders simply lack experience, they can be trained up and unleashed. We're seeing a lot of the latter—pastors and ministry leaders who need training up and unleashing. This has the potential to create disciple-making movements in their churches and communities, and it's exciting. When we say "disciple-making movement," we simply mean any tribe of Jesus followers who join together as force multipliers for the advancement of the kingdom of God throughout the world by making disciples.

A Disciple-Making Tipping Point

When church members start sharing stories of how they're witnessing the power of God in discipleship relationships, it can become a tipping point for them as their church seeks to become a disciple-making community. That's what we need to create a disciple-making movement in the local church. It's one thing for the pastor to preach the discipleship gospel and personally make disciples, but it's an entirely different and greater thing when church members begin sharing their discipleship stories with one another. This is a critical moment in the life of a church, a tipping point of sorts. As author and pastor David Platt has said, "The gospel spreads when every believer makes disciples."[1]

In some ways, a church member's influence on another church member can be far more potent than the pastor's influence. People expect pastors to talk about making disciples (or at least they should expect that). While church members might not say it, they think of discipleship as "the pastor's job" or as "something the pastor should do." They don't, however, expect fellow members to be the great champions of discipleship in the church. But according to the teachings of Jesus, they must.

A number of churches are scattered around America that have reached this tipping point, and they've begun a disciple-making movement in their church. To manage the momentum of such a movement of multiplication, though, we need one more tool: a comprehensive discipleship strategy for the church. In their powerful book, *T4T: A Discipleship Re-Revolution*, authors and church leaders Steve Smith and Ying Kai state that every church should have "a comprehensive process of training believers to witness to the lost and form reproducing discipleship communities generation by generation."[2] This moves us to our next area of focus.

Develop a Comprehensive Strategy

When a church has defined the gospel, knows who a disciple is, has an intentional way of training people to be disciple-making disciples—such as discipleship groups of three and four—and a church's leaders understand the discipleship purpose of all its ministries, the leaders of the church are able to create a truly comprehensive discipleship strategy—an explanation of how a particular church intends to mature and multiply disciples. This strategy makes clear to everyone exactly how they are seeking to fulfill Christ's Great Commission.

The church's discipleship strategy rallies all the church's resources and streamlines everything toward making disciples. As such, it provides a critical decision-making grid, helps to prevent wasting the congregation's sacrificial giving on frivolous things, and makes Jesus' last command to be our first priority. When everything in a local church is streamlined to make disciples, Christ's Great Commission becomes truly great in that church.

It's critical that church leaders don't think of a discipleship strategy as just another program. Francis Chan writes in his book *Multiply,*

> For some of us, our church experience has been so focused on programs that we immediately think about Jesus' command to make disciples in programmatic terms. We expect our church leaders to create some sort of disciple-maker campaign where we sign up, commit to participating for a few months, and then get to cross the Great Commission off our list.[3]

Like Chan says here, discipleship isn't a program, and developing your church's discipleship strategy in the right way will help your church to never forget this.

There's no quick and easy "plug and play" solution for creating a comprehensive discipleship strategy for your church; you can't just adopt another church's discipleship strategy. Every church is unique with its own language, culture, and way of doing things. The work of turning a church from struggling to make disciples into being a thriving disciple-making church isn't easy. In fact, Dallas Willard says it's "very difficult."[4] Looking for quick and easy solutions won't cut it. Our experience has shown us the "discipleship drain" of most churches is badly clogged. The only way to unplug it is for church leaders to roll up their sleeves and begin the deep work of creating a comprehensive discipleship strategy for their congregation.

A New Day of Disciple Making

While some churches have begun to move, an even larger disciple-making movement has started again in America. Hundreds of pastors are already engaged, and the numbers are growing every year. We have seen this in our work with The Bonhoeffer Project, and we know many others who are watching this growth happen all over the country. For us, we take "cohorts" of six to ten pastors and ministry leaders and bring them together once a month during the course of a year. We help them define the gospel in terms of discipleship, and then we teach them how to make disciples in the same way Jesus made disciples. Additionally, we help them create a comprehensive discipleship strategy for their church, and then guide them as they put all these things into practice. It's not a class, a course, or a program; it's an experience of discipleship.

The Bonhoeffer Project is just a few years old, but we're already gaining momentum. In 2015, we saw sixteen cohort members; in 2016, we had sixty-five members; and in 2017, we have had more than one hundred and twenty-five members complete our process! This feels to us like the fourth-soil multiplication that Jesus spoke about in his parable of the sower in Mark 4—thirtyfold, sixtyfold, and hundredfold—praise God!

The new disciple-making movement taking shape is also evident in the growth of the annual National Disciple Making Forum from Discipleship.org. Years ago, this conference was simply a pre-conference option tagged onto another conference with a few hundred participants. In 2017, though, Discipleship.org hosted seventeen disciple-making ministries who are all working together and praying for God to spark a disciple-making movement in America and around the world today. To our knowledge, this is the largest discipleship forum of its kind in the country. In his watershed book, *Experiencing God*, author Henry Blackaby wrote a number of years ago, "Find out where God is at work and join Him there."[5] God is working discipleship back into the church in North America; let's join him there.

Mega vs. Multiplying

If disciple making doesn't multiply disciples, we're doing something wrong. If we are making disciples in the church, we should expect discipleship groups to multiply, church ministries to multiply, servant-leaders within the church to multiply, and our churches themselves to multiply. This type of disciple making and multiplication should impact a church's vision for growth. While this is true, don't assume that just because you begin making disciples, they will multiply. In our consumerist culture, people have been conditioned to receive, not to give. Multiplication requires that disciples are willing to give of themselves for the benefit of others, and this giving is often sacrificial. Unfortunately, the consumerist "receiving" mentality of our culture is often a great hindrance to disciple making in the church. It can also affect a church's vision for growth.

The goal of many churches is to simply get bigger and attract more and more people to attend a Sunday-morning church service. Getting bigger and going to church is good; things should grow. In fact, we're told that the Lord grew the early church very quickly as he "added to their numbers daily those who were being saved" (Acts 2:47). It's a joy when this happens in local churches today, but what will your church do with more people when they come? What's the plan for training them to obey Jesus? What is your vision for growth? Do you have a mega-mindset, a multiplying mindset, or is it something else entirely? These are important questions for everyone in the church to grapple with, especially those on a church's leadership team.

Generally, when a local church begins to grow, the church's leadership team begins spending more time, energy, and money on creating more physical space and adding more programs to attract even more people. We're talking bigger buildings, larger parking lots, and more polished worship services, which is a mega-mindset of church growth. That is, if more people come, then the vision is to get bigger until the church is a "mega-church." Just like a poor man can still be a materialist or addicted to seeking more money, even small churches can have a mega-mindset, set on becoming a larger church.

Contrasting the mega-mindset is the multiplying mindset. Church leaders who have a multiplying mindset hold a vision to grow to a certain size, then multiply, which means sending out disciple-making teams from the church to plant other churches in places the gospel has not yet reached. This requires the new church to immediately and constantly disciple new followers and train members to be servant-leaders. This mindset carries with it a strong expectation for engagement, so get ready to rally your church and add more seats! When a church with this multiplying mindset begins to grow, they cannot simply default to hiring more paid staff members. They will necessarily call equipped and enthusiastic members to step-up.

This type of growth is happening in the global South, where the gospel is advancing in one of the strongest ways in the world right now. For example, churches in South Sudan are embracing the multiplying mindset. Despite being smashed by war and persecution, South Sudanese disciples press on. They are preaching the gospel, making disciples, and planting churches in places without churches, only mosques. God is using men like David Kaya, the pastor of a church in South Sudan's Kajo Keji, to plant more than one hundred churches in the last five years.

David has a "constant" of sorts every Sunday when he calls his congregation to go to new places to plant churches. I (Ben) was with David on one such Sunday when I visited South Sudan. I heard him say, "We must go; we must all be prepared to go; we must obey Jesus' Great Commission and go and make disciples. I'm going to keep on saying this. If you don't like it, leave. But I'm going to keep on telling you to go!" His congregation cheered.

The first time I went to South Sudan was in 2011, when David began his disciple-making work in a new region. I returned in 2015, and the ministry had exponentially multiplied. Now, because of civil war, most of the South Sudanese people are living in large refugee camps; yet, David's teams of trained young men and women are sharing the gospel and making disciples in these camps. By the end of 2017, they had baptized more than two hundred people in a muddy hole. These South Sudanese disciples have a multiplying mindset. They're "going," just like Jesus said. I was inspired, and I hope you are, too.

Everywhere that discipleship is exponentially multiplying in the world, church leaders have a multiplying mindset. After our elders observed with me what these missionaries in South Sudan were doing, our mindset shifted. We were inspired to the point that after forty years, our church reproduced itself for the first time in 2016 and planted a church in a little town just south of us. In 2015, we trained up a small church-planting team of 20 members led by a disciple-making pastor named Mark. As part of Mark's training, he came through The Bonhoeffer Project with me. After just one year, this church plant has become a congregation of forty dedicated souls, and they are already financially self-sufficient. We consider it a joy to bring the gospel to a place where there was no gospel-preaching church in existence. We have just started talking about partnering together to plant another church even further south in another town the gospel has not yet reached. This is an example of how the discipleship gospel is multiplying disciples all over the world.

14

BRINGING IT DOWN TO EARTH

"If you want to bring fundamental change to people's lives and behavior, or change that will persist and influence others, you will need to create a community around them where those new beliefs could be practiced, expressed, and nurtured."

—MALCOLM GLADWELL,
writing about the life of John Wesley

So how do you pull this off in more down-to-earth terms? How does one move from believing a gospel that does not include discipleship to a full-bodied discipleship gospel that includes the broader dimensions of the kingdom of God? Let's get personal.

We want to offer you bits of advice that we believe are fundamental, personal building blocks to move forward once you've fully accepted the seven elements of Jesus' gospel as essential for your life and your message to others.

1. Build Disciple Making Into Your DNA.

The advice "build it into your DNA" seems impossible from the start because DNA is set and unchangeable, isn't it? How does one build anything out of something that is predetermined? Now, there is a difference between physical DNA and the slang we use when we speak of a spiritual DNA, but the principle stands.

God holds us accountable for our actions and he will eventually judge our work according to what we did with what he gave us (1 Cor. 3:10-15). We are also accountable for taking up our calling by faith and action with the grace he has provided us. If this were not so, then Paul would have found no need to exhort Timothy to be strong in grace unless he expected Timothy to exercise his will and act to take hold of grace (2 Tim. 2:1). Building the disciple-making ethos and its practices into your DNA means that you must take your existing spiritual DNA and develop it into Christlike DNA. The New Testament talks about this in terms of a new humanity; Paul says that in Christ, we are a "new creation" (2 Cor. 5:17).

When we say that something is "part of our DNA," we mean it's our bent or our first impulse toward something. Some aspects of our DNA are hard-wired, such as breathing, sweating, laughing, crying, and digestion—all these come as though they were factory-installed in our first nature. Our second nature is primarily learned behavior like patience, love of certain types of food, the enjoyment of nature, physical activity, or having a contemplative disposition. These are acquired by habits that form our character. It is our second nature which builds into our DNA habits and customs that will make spiritual development natural as we become like Christ, especially as we grow in disciple making.

Where to begin with all this?

I (Bill) quite clearly recall a seminar question-and-answer session I was conducting with a group of pastors. There was one pastor in particular who kept voicing objections about changing his church culture from a non-disciple-making ethos to a disciple-making-first focus. We had conducted an exercise in which we asked each pastor to make a list of the people in their churches who would be the best candidates to start a disciple-making journey with them (we ask this question because it's vital to make this type of change with at least one other person, when possible). When we called upon this pastor to report on the list he had made, he told us that the paper for his list was blank. He was emphatic that there was no one, not even one person, in his congregation of two hundred people, who would be interested in discipleship. I was stumped on this one.

"Not one?" I mused with my finger on my chin, reflecting on what I would say next. I knew he believed what he was saying, but I couldn't help but think, *Perhaps he has unconsciously constructed and rationalized his conclusion to protect him from the work he was afraid to do?* Then, I thought, *Or maybe he's afraid because he had no idea what to do.* Then it happened—a Holy Spirit "brainchild." Although it hasn't happened very often to me, I've learned to recognize it when it appears.

So I said, "May I ask you a question?" I thought permission would be important for what I was about to say. He consented.

"How about you?" I asked. "Are you interested in discipleship? When you say that there is no one to do this with you, aren't you at least that one person who wants a fresh start to rebuild your ministry and develop a congregation centered on making disciples?"

He was befuddled by my question, mumbled that he didn't know, and sat down.

Disciple making hadn't become part of this pastor's "DNA," so he couldn't begin, and he didn't know what to do. And when you don't know what to do, you do what you know how to do—go online and order a program with materials and videos. You'll just keep running programs, one after the other, until the congregation finally refuses to participate because they see little life change and no multiplication. This is one reason some churches die.

This explains the reason that so many lead pastors insulate and delegate. They insulate themselves from the congregational life of discipleship, which they most often do by delegating the actual work of discipleship to staff or laity. We agree that delegation is good. However, lead pastors need to be involved in disciple making, too. The DNA of their ministry was developed in seminary or in a church subculture that too often values consumption, production, and the rewards that come with mega-ministry growth 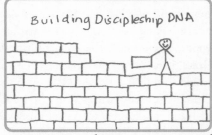 metrics. This is not an intentional or even a conscious decision; it just sort of grows on churches like moss grows on rocks—slowly and over time, until it takes over the whole thing. So we must evaluate where we're at and where we need to go.

We leave you with a few simple exhortations for going about implementing this type of DNA change in your life:

- Find various types of people who have a discipleship-first mentality and spend time talking with them if you know them, read their publications (if you know about them), and learn more directly from others.[1]
- Search the Scriptures and study Jesus' ways and means of discipleship.
- Pray for wisdom from God on how to move forward.

When you come to the point where for you to do anything other than to make disciples is a grievous sin, then you'll know that you have the disciple-making-first DNA. Remember, this is about your personal preparation to lead a disciple-making movement—when you call out, "Follow me!" you will want to know where you're leading them and what you'll do on the way.

2. Develop a Satisfied Soul

Every time I (Bill) read Psalm 23, I wince at the words, "The Lord is my shepherd, I have all that I need." I don't doubt that the Lord is my shepherd; I just know my experience doesn't always fit that description. Sometimes, I need a lot of stuff! I suppose my restless and aggressive nature makes it difficult to follow my leader to rest in green meadows and sit beside peaceful streams. As the more traditional translations claim, the green meadows and peaceful streams will "restore my soul." This seems to be great advice if you're a sheep in the ancient Near East, but I am a driven man living in twenty-first century America.

"To restore" something means to return it to its original condition. And by definition, that would mean a satisfied soul because originally our ancestors, Adam and Eve, were satisfied. If we want to have a satisfied soul, we need to address the problem that French physicist and theologian Blaise Pascal presents when he says, "The whole calamity of man comes from one single thing, that he cannot keep quiet in a room."[2] He's talking about the difficulty of stopping to think, to be alone, and to not be distracted. To resist distraction is a skill, and developing that skill requires training.

Another challenge is that acquiring a satisfied soul doesn't become attractive until it's too late—when you're about to collapse. The satisfied soul doesn't come from having the best-looking girl, the fastest car with the biggest rush, or the most exotic vacation.

The idea of seeking soul satisfaction tends to make people drowsy. It isn't a word that describes accomplishment, and not many medals are given for its heroic acts. A satisfied person is normally someone who pushes back from the dinner table at peace because there is no conflict around them.

If Jesus is our model and our leader, and we are to become like him, we must go beyond culturally tainted views of a satisfied person. Jesus' life was crammed with conflict. His ministry years were tumultuous; he was on the run or in hiding as a marked man, and he was always in danger. Still, Jesus taught us and continues to teach us how we might live in the crucible that is life and yet be at peace with God. When you're at peace with God, your mind and spirit can live, like the Psalmist says, beside quiet waters and be nourished in green meadows. You can serve with inner peace even when your enemies surround you. Sometimes those enemies are actual people; other times, they are anxieties about the past or the future, or about events real or imagined.

The most common anxieties that destroy our satisfaction are the common metrics that culture uses to determine our value. When we don't measure up, we are in distress. Jesus phrases the power and difficulty of taking this approach so beautifully:

> The Kingdom of God is like a farmer who scatters seed on the ground. Night and day, while he's asleep or awake, the seed sprouts and grows, but he does not understand how it happens. The earth produces the crops on its own. First a leaf blade pushes through, then the heads of wheat are formed, and finally the grain ripens. And as soon as the grain is ready, the farmer comes and harvests it with a sickle, for the harvest time has come.
>
> —MARK 4:26-29

I am sure that we don't know exactly the nature of how spiritual birth and growth actually happens. We know that, like the farmer, we have a role to play in both, but something very mysterious takes place that is out of our hands and beyond our reach. It is for this reason that we stop, that we rest, and that we linger in God's presence. As a disciple-making leader, you sow the seed, you watch the field, and you pray for rain, sunshine, and proper conditions. You put a scarecrow in the field, you irrigate, you pray for growth, and you use all your skill. But in the end, you go into your house and wait, you pray, you hope. And once in a while, you look out the window, and when it's time, you strike. You fire up the combine, you prepare your equipment, you plan your strategy, and you begin the harvest. As you sit atop your great harvest machine, you can't help but wonder, *How did this happen?* and you will never really know.

Meditate on God to Satisfy Your Soul

Whether or not you're a pastor, the work of making disciples is long and arduous. The length of time this work takes means that while we can give you ideas on how to begin, finishing the task is for you and the Holy Spirit. First, schedule a period of time—two or three days a week—to hide from people, machines, and work-related issues, and then face yourself in the presence of God alone. Jesus spent a lot of his time trying to get away from people; be his disciple in this way and excel at it. This could be thirty minutes or one hour. When you get away, just sit there or stand or kneel. Whatever you do, don't say or do anything for some time; just practice listening to your own head. Of course, this will be hard. Now, you can pray or quote scripture, but be otherwise silent and practice being in a room alone with God for an extended period of time.

Consider how the world moves on without you, how others accomplish work without you. Think about how few people actually think about your disciple-making work, how much of a privilege it is to work, to matter, and to make a difference. This is just the detox period, where we learn to live without the noise, the beeps, the pings, the sing-song ringtones, and the ridiculous notion that being online and available makes you important. Don't be legalistic about the whole thing. Instead, relax. Learn how to pray again and to think deeply, and you will find that you will become the kind of person who has something to say.

For some of you, developing this type of soul satisfaction is a foreign concept. Let me (Bill) give you a pointer on what it means to glorify God and magnify his Holy Name, to behold his beauty: don't focus in your head, but

use your head. If you're anything like me, you may be confused when someone tells you to, "Go sit under a tree and enjoy God." I've heard people quite sincerely and full of passion speak about how they "beheld God's beauty." I don't doubt their authenticity, but I've often wondered, *What are they talking about? What did they see and where did they see it?* I've been around a bit, and I could make an educated guess. I think they're speaking of being moved by a thought, a Scriptural passage, a certain memory, or a special experience. My point here is to encourage you to not try too hard for a special, earth-moving experience when you're sitting under that tree. Listen for the Lord, even if it takes some time.

I've learned that to magnify the Lord, to behold his beauty, starts with observing what's around me. For example, the tree. You're sitting in its shade, leaning on its trunk for support, and God created that tree. Then, move to the grass, and on to the sky, the sun, the clouds, the wind, and the wildlife. If you're in the midst of hills or mountains, behold them and marvel at God. As you start to marvel in all that God has created, you magnify him. This focused practice should lead to some form of praise and thanksgiving along with a genuinely insightful perspective on life. You may, for example, be able to use this practice to meditate on the truth that Jesus is holding this whole enterprise together. Don't feel the pressure to make something up or to have "holy thoughts." Relax. You just might become a contemplative yet.

Developing a Well-Ordered Life

We believe the tips below will radically change your life, but only pursue them if you're willing to do what it takes to make significant progress. These tips are especially relevant for knowledge workers, pastors, or those who work directly with producing ideas. Train yourself to do the following:

- Do the hard stuff first
- Exercise daily
- Don't read email until after lunch
- Don't answer your phone before noon
- Don't have an open door policy—it will ruin your life
- Spend the first four hours of your day praying, reading, studying, and reflecting
- Plan your week and stick to it, even if you think it might kill you

Work on these things, and you'll start to see your fragmented mind experience a new wholeness. Plus, you'll restore your ability to concentrate. When you open your mouth, what comes out will be more thought out and significantly more important and helpful.

I (Bill) also suggest that you don't read too much, especially the hip, leading-edge, and really short books out there. Too much reading will actually distract you from knowing anything in depth. You can't know everything, so ask yourself what you're called to know. Obey your calling and don't just half-know your subject. Instead, know it fully and keep digging in the same hole. That way, you'll learn the secrets of the earth.

All of these things may seem unconnected to discipleship, but this is where it begins—with you. When you become a different kind of person—one who is truly following Jesus with your whole life—you'll be able to make disciples more easily. If your soul is satisfied and your life is well-ordered, then you're in a good place. You've also set yourself up to resist distraction from the most important work of multiplying disciples.

3. Get Some Disciples

You cannot create a disciple-making movement all by yourself or try to do it by "going it alone." You can, however, create a disciple-making movement by getting some disciples. You'll need your own disciples—evidence that you have the discipleship-first DNA. Choose carefully who will join you on this journey because this trip will be long with causalities. Ask faithful people to join you, those who are also willing to learn to teach others (2 Tim. 2:2). While they will eventually teach others, you must first teach them.

You may recall the conversion of Saul, the self-described chief persecutor of Christians, to Apostle Paul (he was called "Saul" until after his conversion). The Lord had directed him to go to Damascus and find a man named Ananias. When they met, Ananias spoke God's word to Paul, and he was filled with the Holy Spirit. Scales fell from his eyes, and he was baptized. Paul began to preach, and he was both compelling and irrefutable. The tables had turned, and Saul the persecutor had become Paul the persecuted. Saul was passionate about punishing Christians, and now he was just as passionate about proclaiming the gospel, even if that meant being punished for serving Christ. He was popular with some, but hated by others. We know this story fairly well, but after his conversion, when he was facing persecution, his disciples stepped up to help him out.

As the story goes, the religious Jews in Damascus were plotting to kill him (you get the idea that this story takes place a few weeks, possibly even months, after Paul's conversion). In response to the plot against him, Paul's friends agreed that he needed to leave the city to escape. Apparently, the gates were being watched, so one night Paul was lowered in a basket over the wall, allowing him to escape. I (Bill) have always found it important at this point in the story that the people on the other end of the rope were his disciples.[3] After Paul was gone from Damascus, the gospel remained and so did a community of disciples. While some disciples preceded Paul (such as Ananias), many became disciples as a direct result of Paul's preaching. Naturally, we ask, "Who are your disciples?" Choose wisely because eventually you will need partners, comrades in arms.

Write down a few names of potential disciples, not many—just five or less. Pray over these people and make a checklist of qualities you're looking for in disciples. Consider the following list of what we consider to be the first and most important qualities:

- Hungry to learn, not just content
- Has ministry skills
- Willing to replicate
- Willing to teach others
- Proven faithfulness
- Available—regardless of their ability or likability; if they are unavailable, then all their great qualities don't matter
- Willing to be criticized, lose friends, have family members get angry with them, or be embarrassed for the sake of the gospel
- Willing to change their personal schedule, even vacation plans, to keep commitments
- Willing to lead others and work with you for several spiritual generations

We recommend that you make a written covenant, but make sure you're willing to sign it before you present it to others. Sometimes, whether we're paid professionals or lay leaders, we forget to personalize such things for ourselves. Too often we leave people behind in the middle of discipling them because we got a "better opportunity." Plan to spend one year with these chosen ones. Stay in relationship with them, though, because when they start leading, they'll need you more than ever.

15

DEVELOPING YOUR PLAN

The temptation for us, as this book's authors, is to give you a step-by-step plan. We will resist this temptation, though, because a prescribed list of instructions would do you harm. We don't want to create disciple-making zombies out of you. We suggest making a plan—your own plan—because we want your work to be fully human and fully personal within your context.

The common virus among writers and powerful practitioners is to present you, the reader, with a ready-made solution. We're going to insist that you do this for yourself. We could inject you with a factory-made, synthetic plan, but you can develop your own plan through prayer, study, and reflection, and actualize it by carefully living it out. So how do you create your own plan? If you're starting from scratch, this can be a daunting task, but don't lose heart! Jesus promises to be with us always, until the end, if we're making disciples (Matt. 28:20). We've devoted this chapter to the important task of helping you create a workable plan.

You can't make disciples without some sort of accountability, and you can't practice accountability without structure. That's where a plan comes

in. Accountability is simply helping people keep their commitments to God. You don't want to force anything, but you can create a supportive environment where people who have made commitments to God can more easily keep them. The majority of people give up on themselves too soon in the discipleship process they have chosen because of discouragement. Caring persons, though, provide encouragement and exhort their friends to continue, especially when it's difficult. The very best people at accountability are on the same journey as the people they keep accountable. They have similar challenges and move forward in following Jesus together.

Start with Your Congregation

The most common pastoral malady in the Western hemisphere is laboring under the false belief that congregants agree on the gospel and what it means. Our guess is you get that by now. The most common gospels make discipleship and serious Christian faith optional and disconnected from going to heaven when you die. The pastor's hands are tied by the basic assumptions of what most congregants believe is required of them. *Ipso facto*, pastors spend much of their career persuading nominal or consumeristic professors of Christian dogma to take up the option on their salvation contract.

This will require the leader to carefully reteach the gospel point by point to the congregation. Of course, this requires care and concern, reassuring members that they're safe while this is all rethought and reconsidered.

One tip that might help: don't trash the gospel you have been teaching and previous generations have taught. Simply cut the taproot and don't nourish and feed it any longer. Rebuild around it and explain it in such a way that creates a more robust gospel in a way that will help people flourish and understand that their calling to salvation is also a call to discipleship—no exceptions, no excuses. Additionally, all followers of Jesus are to make other followers of Jesus. This is our calling, the full and abundant life to which Christ has called us (John 10:10).[1]

Remember the Goal

It's easy to forget that included in Christ's teachings are the commands to fill the earth with Christlikeness and to preach the gospel of the kingdom to every nation. While the church gathers for discipleship, it is also sent into the

world to love the world like Christ loved it. We're called to spread disciples and disciple makers to every nation.

This will require a significant change in the mindset of most pastors and congregational members because neither generally expect this much from church members. It's a substantial upgrade from the norm to expect every member to become a disciple maker. This is about much more than simple service to the church through church programs on the church campus. Instead, this is about one's complete life, especially when we're not at church.

This brings up that sticky question, "Why don't churches require discipleship for membership?" The reason is because it would be impossible to enforce. Christians function largely on the honor system, kind of like how golfers keep score. Christians keep their own score and call penalties on themselves when they break a rule. Traditionally, we call it confession of sins. Catholics actually do a better job than most here, because they require confession before communion. Even this, though, is based on the honor system I would venture to say that at least a few people have lied to a priest. Raising expectations and appealing to ordinary Christians to answer in full the call of Christ should be normative for those who believe the gospel. But it must be instilled into the basic understanding of what it means to be saved today. The reason, as we have argued throughout this book, starts with theology. However, there's also a practical side to this, as well.

Even after you're convinced of the discipleship gospel, how do you move forward? As you make plans, it starts with a new metric for success.

Use the New Metric of Success

The most common metrics for defining success in the church today are buildings, dollars, and seats. Clearly, we need new metrics for success. For example, we should measure success by how many activated disciples inhabit a geographic space, not by how many churches are in that same space. Taking this mindset with you as you exit the holy ground on which your church gathers each Sunday, you'll know that every disciple is a mobilized, Spirit-filled ambassador for Christ (2 Cor. 5:15-21).

The issue is not how many churches are in the Los Angeles area (where Bill lives), and it's not about the number of attendees when you combine worship services. The important metric is answering the question, "How many fully activated disciples are living in Los Angeles?" When it comes to fulfilling the Great Commission, this is the metric that matters, the mandate that Jesus gave us two thousand years ago.

Some of us "active types" live, work, and play in virtually every domain of culture. What we may not understand is that while we play in one hundred places, Christ always plays in ten thousand places. In the government (city, state, national), the entertainment business, public schools, courts, universities—we are everywhere. Your plan, then, should be shaped and evaluated by how effective it is at deploying well-trained, Spirit-filled members into all domains of culture. It needs to go beyond reproduction and include multiplication. The difference is simple: reproduction is one person reproducing in another person. Multiplication is when gospel DNA is passed along to that second person, and they, along with the first person, believe that their new life in Christ continues on to be multiple reproductions—leading to several spiritual generations.

Develop Your Planning Worksheet

The worksheet is an opportunity to put on paper what you really believe and how you plan to implement it. Remember, if you don't have a plan, you don't intend to do it. While your discipleship plan can include many items, we want to give you a basic framework of three questions you can use to fill in the "meat" of your plan. The three questions are who, how, and what?

1. Who is a disciple"?

Your definition of a disciple must be specific enough for you to answer the next question: how do you make a disciple? For example, let's say you define a disciple as someone who has five characteristics, something like:

- Develops a conversational relationship with God through the Word and prayer
- Reveals Christ every day by bearing fruit
- Responds to God through daily obedience
- Has joy and is contented in spirit
- Loves others as Christ loved others

How to grow a person with these characteristics will likely require specific spiritual exercises and activities in a community of kindred spirits who all want the same qualities developed in them. You can develop all these activities, but first make sure you know what your end goal is by clearly defining what a disciple looks like based on your understanding of Scripture.

2. How will you make disciples?

Once you've defined the "who," you can answer the "how." Answering this question requires you to think about how to group people, determine activities, provide leadership training, and make decisions about schedules, goals, and other organizational aspects. The difficult work is identifying each characteristic, then naming an action or activity done in community that will create the desired trait. Take, for example, the characteristic that a disciple reveals Christ daily by bearing fruit. You must create opportunities for your group members for them to experience bearing fruit. It doesn't just happen; you need a plan. There is a much higher probability that your people will learn service by actually serving rather than by merely contemplating service. This was the reason Jesus traveled with his disciples rather than hold a continual retreat like the Essences, first-century Jews who lived near the Dead Sea (far away from society) to maintain their holy huddle. Instead, teach your disciples *how to do the activities that are necessary to become the type of people who follow everything that Jesus commanded.*

3. What will these disciples do?

Describe how the world around you will be impacted if your quest to make many more disciples succeeds. How will you know the plan worked? Write your plan in pencil with an eraser nearby because you'll need to keep working on it and changing it—sometimes daily—until it's the helpful tool that you need. Whatever you have planned and are trusting God for in general, stick with it to the end!

EPILOGUE

At the time of writing this book, Eugene Peterson had just recently decided to retire from public life at the age of eighty-four. No longer will he take speaking assignments, and he will no longer write books. Alas, he has written his last book, *As Kingfishers Catch Fire: A Conversation on the Ways of God Formed by the Words of God*. At the age of 70, I (Bill) am now fourteen years younger than Peterson, but I do not assume that I will have fourteen more years—even fourteen more minutes! Every word I write may be my last, so allow me to counsel you, my younger readers.

Jesus is the most important and most beautiful thing that has happened to this world. God has visited us and set a plan for us to follow. Ben and I have endeavored to present our understanding of that plan here. After all, God has not promised to bless *our* plan or *our* dreams, but he has said he would be with us all the way if we are dedicated to *his plan* (Matt. 28:20). He stated that plan simply to his disciples, and by this point, they knew what he was asking them to do. When Jesus said, "Make disciples of all nations [that is, ethnic groups]," they understood that he meant they were to do with others what he had been doing with them for the last few years. They didn't have to ask questions about what he wanted them to do because they had seen it done; they were trained and ready to go.

The Church Today Waits

In contrast with the original disciples of Jesus, the contemporary church has many questions about what it means to "make disciples." It is common for pastors and other leaders to admit they don't have any experience in disciple making and that they don't know how to lead others in it. As a church culture, we haven't made disciples for such a long time in history that it has become normal to *not* make disciples. If we have been making disciples, we haven't been making them consistently enough to make it normative. In addition to the rarity of discipleship practices, even our gospel has been corrupted. It has been reduced, watered down, and has become a hindrance to the very thing Jesus wants us to do. He wants to make disciples who make disciples who still make more disciples, *ad infinitum*.

The contemporary false gospels we've defined are non-discipleship gospels that have changed the goal that Jesus gave us. They have changed the making of disciples to the making of converts and have separated evangelism from disciple making. These gospels (and our penchant to follow them) have overlooked and disregarded the imperative to teach every disciple to obey what Christ commanded, a component that includes making other disciples. The false gospels we've created don't include living the life of Christ as he lived, nor have they included engagement in mission as a normative practice for believers. As we have made clear in this volume, the gospels floating around today have dismissed from the gospel the *follow me* part of Jesus' call to salvation. The evidence of salvation is someone who has heard the call of Jesus—follow me, learn from me, serve me, die for me, listen to me—and responded with obedience. The contemporary non-discipleship gospels have done great damage to the cause of Christ.

Have we cracked the code here? Meaning, have we now explained the discipleship gospel, also known as "the gospel of the kingdom," in such a way that you can work with it? We can't lay claim to such an accomplishment, nor should we, because that would be foolishness. But we will say that we have delivered to you something that will make you think and something that will be a pathway to transform your understanding of the gospel and help you teach those you lead. We hope that what we have done here will unleash your people to believe that they can make disciples who will indeed make even more disciples.

Dietrich Bonhoeffer and the Gospel Today

The content of this book is vital for the church today. We know the potential impact of a proper understanding of the gospel because of the example of a young, influential German theologian, Dietrich Bonhoeffer (the inspiration for the name of our organization, The Bonhoeffer Project).

By the early twentieth century, the non-discipleship gospel had failed Germany, reflecting on the dead orthodoxy of what used to be. That gospel had even failed to reach the young Dietrich Bonhoeffer. It has had the same effect on millions today in nearly every nation of the world. In the modern Western civilization, we have tried hard to make the gospel easy to believe and even easier to acquire. But today's easy-to-believe gospels don't resonate with the deep cry of our souls. They just amuse us—for a while.

We need what finally reached Bonhoeffer: a full-bodied gospel filled with passion and social justice from the Abyssinian Baptist Church. This is the kind of message that engaged Bonhoeffer while he was living in New York City. It was a gospel that required following Jesus, one that expected people to show this transformation by their lives. Bonhoeffer returned to Germany a changed man.

He soon engaged in the struggle against Adolf Hitler and his Nazi war machine, spending the last two years of his life in prison. On the day of his execution, a camp doctor, H. Fischer-Hullstrung, recorded his impression of Bonhoeffer just prior to his execution:

> On the morning of that day between five and six o'clock, the prisoners were taken from their cells. The verdict of the court martial was read to them. Through the half-open door in one room of the huts, I saw Pastor Bonhoeffer before taking off his garb, kneeling on the floor praying fervently to his God. I was most deeply moved by the way this loveable man prayed, so devout and so certain that God heard his prayer. At the place of execution, he again said a short prayer and then climbed the steps to the gallows, brave and composed. His death ensued after a few seconds. In the almost fifty years that I worked as a doctor, I have hardly ever seen a man die so entirely submissive to the will of God.[1]

We read what Fischer-Hullstrung observed in Bohoeffer, a man who didn't just write about denying himself, taking up his cross, and following Jesus; he actually lived it—even in death. Bonhoeffer was willing to follow Jesus to the very end with neither conditions nor excuses, and we must be willing to follow Jesus to the end, too.

The life of Bonhoeffer is connected to his beliefs about the nature and effect of the gospel that Jesus preached. He writes, "The only person who can be justified by grace alone is the person who has left all to follow Christ. Such a person knows that the call to discipleship is a gift of grace and that the call is inseparable from grace."[2]

A Final Word

I (Bill) can't finish this book without sharing a conversation I had with an eighty-nine-year-old giant of the disciple-making movement, Dr. Robert Coleman, the author of *The Master Plan of Evangelism*.

I asked Dr. Coleman, "If you could only ask the American church one question, what would it be?"

He didn't pause long before he said, "What is your excuse for not obeying our Lord's command to make disciples?"

Reflecting on his question, I think their excuse is that no one told them they were responsible to make disciples and that no one taught them to be a disciple. No one told them that discipleship was part of what it means to be saved and to be faithful—that as ordinary believers, there was such a high expectation for them.

I think they do have an excuse, and that excuse is the leaders who have failed them. If you're a pastor, the issue is even deeper because the people you lead think it's your job to reach the world for Christ. They won't change their minds until you change yours. Their excuse is real, and it's us, the leaders of the church—pastors and lay leaders alike. We have failed to teach them correctly, to lead them by example, and to create environments for discipleship. We have failed to equip them to make it all a reality. Oh yes, it has happened now and then throughout history, but it has been largely lost. Now, it is being discovered once again. Our prayer is that this book may, in some way, be a part of that renaissance.

NOTES

Introduction

1. Bill has written on this topic extensively in *Conversion and Discipleship* (Grand Rapids: Zondervan, 2016).

Chapter 1

1. For more about the kingdom in the life of Jesus, see the works of scholars such as N.T. Wright in *Jesus and the Victory of God* (Minneapolis: Fortress Press, 1996); Scot McKnight in *The King Jesus Gospel* (Grand Rapids: Zondervan, 2011); *Kingdom Conspiracy: Returning to the Radical Mission of the Local Church* (Grand Rapids: Baker Books, 2014); and George Eldon Ladd, *The Gospel of the Kingdom: Scriptural Studies in the Kingdom of God* (Grand Rapids: Eerdmans Publishing, 1959). Examples in the New Testament: Matthew 3:2; 6:33; Mark 1:15; Luke 4:45; and John 3:5.
2. For passages about how God's kingdom restores all creation, see Psalm 145: 8-13; Mark 1:15; and Matthew 6:9-10.
3. For more about how eternal life begins in our present life in the kingdom, see Mark 10:30; John 3:3, 36; 10:10.
4. In his book, *Salvation by Allegiance Alone: Rethinking Faith, Works, and the Gospel of Jesus the King*, Dr. Matthew Bates claims, "Faith in

Jesus is best described as allegiance to him as King" (Grand Rapids: Baker Academic, 2017) 77.

5. Matthew's Gospel uses the phrase "kingdom of heaven," while Mark and Luke use "kingdom of God." Both phrases refer to the same reality.
6. Dietrich Bonhoeffer, *The Cost of Discipleship* (New York: Touchstone, 1995) 59.
7. It should be noted that Jesus had spent over three years teaching his disciples about the kingdom of God as something near them, within them, and not primarily of this world. He taught that it would, however, gradually come to the world and eventually come in full regalia after his return and the judgment.
8. For Elijah and Elisha's story, see 2 Kings 6:8-22. Jesus fulfilled this through the apostles, who went to the nations.
9. For a complete treatment of this subject, see the Introduction and Chapter 1 of *Conversion and Discipleship* (Grand Rapids: Zondervan, 2016).
10. Bill is cofounder with Brandon Cook of The Bonhoeffer Project, which is devoted to creating disciple-making movements in local contexts. Ben helps Bill as they train ministry leaders toward this end.
11. From a personal conversation Dallas Willard had with Bill.
12. This is a summary of Kierkegaard's thoughts by Stephen Backhouse in *Kierkegaard, A Single Life* (Grand Rapids: Zondervan, 2016) 151.

Chapter 2

1. C.H. Dodd, *The Apostolic Preaching & Its Developments* (New York: Harper & Row, 1964) 76.
2. *Conversion and Discipleship* (Grand Rapids: Zondervan, 2016) 33.

Chapter 3

1. For the reasoning that Mark was the first Gospel written, see John F. Walvoord and Roy B. Zuck's *The Bible Knowledge Commentary* (Wheaton: Victor Books) 99.
2. This is a phrase used by Matthew Bates to describe the declarative elements of the gospel. Such a phrase helps us distinguish between, in the language of this book, the four declarative statements of the gospel

and the three imperative responses, all of which are essential to the gospel. For more on this, see Matthew W. Bates, *Salvation By Allegiance Alone: Rethinking Faith, Works, and the Gospel of Jesus the King* (Grand Rapids: Baker Academic, 2017) 29.

3. Scot McKnight, *King Jesus Gospel: The Original Good News Revisited* (Grand Rapids: Zondervan, 2011) 58.
4. Henry M. Haley, *Haley's Bible Handbook* (Grand Rapids: Zondervan, 1965) 475.
5. Gary R. Habermas and Michael R. Licona do excellent work extrapolating these things in their book *The Case for the Resurrection of Jesus* (Grand Rapids: Kregel Publications, 2004).
6. Ibid. 52-53.
7. *The King Jesus Gospel* (Grand Rapids: Zondervan, 2011) 51.
8. *The Divine Conspiracy: Rediscovering Our Hidden Life in God* (New York: HarperCollins, 1998) xvii.

Chapter 4

1. A.F. Buzzard, *The Coming Kingdom of the Messiah* (Wyoming: Ministry School Publications, 1988) 14-16.
2. George Eldon Ladd, *The Gospel of the Kingdom of God: Scriptural Studies in the Kingdom of God* (Grand Rapids: Eerdmans, 1959) 11.
3. For more information on cohorts of The Bonhoeffer Project, visit www. thebonhoefferproject.com.
4. George Eldon Ladd made this language popular in his book *The Gospel of the Kingdom of God: Scriptural Studies in the Kingdom of God* (Grand Rapids: Eerdmans, 1959) 59.

Chapter 5

1. See also John 3:16.
2. Matthew W. Bates, *Salvation By Allegiance Alone: Rethinking Faith, Works, and the Gospel of Jesus the King* (Grand Rapids: Baker Academic, 2017) 77.
3. Ibid.
4. Ibid. 8.

Chapter 6

1. As part of our research for this book, we emailed Dr. Gary Habermas, a leading expert on Jesus' resurrection, and asked him if he knew of another event in ancient history with more historical evidence than Christ's resurrection. He graciously replied, "It's certainly possible that some other event has more evidence, but I can't think what it might be!"
2. The word "excruciating" was created to describe the intense pain of crucifixion. If you look closely at the root of the word, it has crucifixion at its center.
3. See www.opendoorsusa.org for more information on modern-day martyrdom.
4. Romans 6:11; 8:11 (emphasis ours).
5. N.T. Wright, *The Day the Revolution Began: Reconsidering the Meaning of Jesus' Crucifixion* (New York: HarperOne, 2016).
6. We are not going to get into the theological depths of all these aspects of Christ's cross here. There are plenty of good resources that do that, including John R. W. Stott's *The Cross of Christ* (Downers Grove: InterVarsity Press, 1986).
7. Dallas Willard, "Spiritual Formation as a Natural Part of Salvation," lecture presented at the Wheaton Theology Conference, 2009.

Chapter 7

1. The idea of *inheriting eternal life* is used interchangeably with the concepts of *entering the kingdom of God* and *being saved* by Jesus and his apostles (Mark 10:17, 23, 26).
2. Galatians 5:17; John 15:4.
3. The phrase "first mention" is a technical term that relates to the principle of "first mention" in biblical hermeneutics, which says that the first mention of a particular concept in the Bible (i.e., good works) in many ways defines the foundational meaning of that concept throughout the whole Bible.
4. Dietrich Bonhoeffer, *The Cost of Discipleship* (New York: Touchstone, 1995) 45.

Chapter 8

1. Global Discipleship Initiative seminar at Camerillo Community Church, March 27-29, 2017.
2. Some advocates of non-repentance gospels use Acts 15:19 to assert that repentance is adding a needless obstacle to the gospel. They argue the "trouble" to which James refers here includes repentance. This is a clearly flawed interpretation for two reasons. First, the trouble had to do with whether or not Gentiles needed to be circumcised to be saved. Repentance wasn't the "trouble," though, circumcision was. Second, James describes the Gentiles being saved as "those who *turn* to God." That's repentance! To "turn to God" is to repent of sin. Acts 15:19 can't be used to argue that repentance is a burden to new believers. It's actually teaching that repentance is a blessing of salvation.
3. From the Foreword of Aldous Huxley's *Brave New World* (New York: Harper & Brothers Publishers, 1932).
4. Thomas Cahill, *The Gift of the Jews: How a Tribe of Desert Nomads Changed the Way Everyone Thinks and Feels* (New York: Anchor Books, 1998) 63.

Chapter 9

1. From a presentation in 2008 at Wheaton College by Dallas Willard called, "Scripture Formation as a Natural Part of Salvation."
2. Scot McKnight, *King Jesus Gospel* (Grand Rapids: Zondervan, 2011) 58.
3. Some might argue that the gospel is revealed through creation. While in a most general sense this is true, the gospel is specifically about Jesus being revealed as the Christ. Because creation, in general, doesn't reveal this, we have left it off this list.
4. There are other specific passages in the New Testament that define the gospel, like Romans 1:1-6, which are similar to 1 Corinthians 15:3-4. We treat 1 Corinthians 15:3-4 as representative of all these other succinct articulations of the gospel in the New Testament.
5. Matthew W. Bates, *Salvation by Allegiance Alone* (Grand Rapids: Baker Academic, 2017) 205-206.
6. As we noted earlier, a more complete explanation of the five non-discipleship gospels can be found in Bill Hull's *Conversion and Discipleship* (Grand Rapids: Zondervan, 2016) 32-40.

7. Matthew 23:15. Perhaps there is a direct correlation between the double-curse Paul called down in Galatians 1:6-9 and Jesus' statement that the Pharisees' disciples were "twice as much a child of hell" as they were in Matthew 23:15.

8. Tim Keller, "The Gospel in All its Forms," Acts29.com, May 23, 2008, http://www.acts29.com/tim-keller-explains-the-gospel.

9. Our friend Greg Ogden does a masterful job of showing that Paul's language of spiritual parenting is an expression of Jesus' language of disciple making in his book *Transforming Discipleship: Making Disciples a Few at a Time* (Downers Grove: IVP Books, 2016) Chapter 5.

10. Collin Marshall and Tony Payne, *The Trellis and the Vine: The Ministry Mind-Shift that Changes Everything* (Kingsford: Matthias Media, 2009) 147.

Chapter 10

1. From a private conversation in 2002 between Bill and Dallas Willard.

2. Greg Ogden, *Transforming Discipleship: Making Disciples a Few at a Time* (Downers Grove: InterVarsity Press, 2016) 68.

3. For more information about cohorts of The Bonhoeffer Project, please visit www.thebonhoefferproject.com.

4. Bill Hull, *The Disciple-Making Pastor: Leading Others on the Journey of Faith* (Grand Rapids: Baker Books, 2007) 21-22.

Chapter 11

1. Eugene Peterson, *A Long Obedience in the Same Direction: Discipleship in an Instant Society* (Downers Grove: IVP, 2000.)

2. Greg Ogden, *Transforming Discipleship: Making Disciples a Few at a Time* (Downers Grove: IVP Books, 2016) 74.

3. Craig Etheredge, *Invest in a Few: Giving Your Life to What Matters Most* (Discipleship.org: 2017) 62. To download this free eBook, visit www.discipleship.org/ebooks.

4. See also Matthew 1:1; Mark 1:1; and John 20:20-21.

5. Ben Sobels and Bill Hull, *The Discipleship Gospel Workbook: Multiply Disciples with the Gospel of Mark* (Nashville: HIM Publications, 2018), available at www.himpublications.com.

6. Mark 4:35; 5:1; 5:21.

Chapter 12

1. Scot McKnight, *The King Jesus Gospel* (Grand Rapids: Zondervan, 2011) 18.
2. Eugene Peterson, "Doing the Right Thing in the Wrong Way," Spiritual Formation Forum Conference, May 2004, Bill's personal notes.

Chapter 13

1. David Platt, *Follow Me: A Call to Die. A Call to Live.* (Carol Stream: Tyndale House Publishers, 2013) xi.
2. Steve Smith with Ying Kai, *T4T: A Discipleship Re-Revolution* (Monument: WIGTake Resources, 2011) 44.
3. Francis Chan with Mark Beaving, *Multiply: Disciples Making Disciples* (Colorado Springs: David C. Cook, 2012) 31.
4. From a presentation in 2008 at Wheaton College by Dallas Willard called, "Spiritual Formation as a Natural Part of Salvation."
5. Henry and Richard Blackaby and Claude King, *Experiencing God: Knowing and Doing the Will of God*, Revised and Expanded (Nashville: B&H Books, 2008) 82.

Chapter 14

1. Find a description of the disciple-making-pastor DNA in *Conversion and Discipleship* (Grand Rapids: Zondervan, 2016) 205.
2. As found in A.G. Sertillanges's *The Intellectual Life: Its Spirit, Conditions, Methods*, trans. Mary Ryan (Washington D.C.: The Catholic University of America Press, 1987) 216.
3. Acts 9:25 says, "his disciples."

Chapter 15

1. For a full explanation of the various gospels that are presently taught, see *Conversion and Discipleship* (Grand Rapids: Zondervan, 2016) 33.

Epilogue

1. Eric Metaxas, *Bonhoeffer, Pastor, Prophet, Martyr, Spy* (Nashville: Thomas Nelson, 2010) 532.
2. *The Cost of Discipleship* (New York: Touchstone, 1995) 51.

ABOUT THE AUTHORS

BILL HULL has devoted his adult life to pastoring, teaching, and writing about Christ's command to make disciples. His primary means for pursuing his mission as a discipleship evangelist has been through pastoring for twenty years, teaching in more than fifty countries around the world, and authoring more than twenty-five books. Bill is now the leader of The Bonhoeffer Project, which is devoted to the creation of disciple-making leaders. You can learn more about his work at TheBonhoefferProject.com and BillHull.net.

BEN SOBELS grew up in Australia, but in his early twenties came to America to caddie for a good friend who is a professional golfer. During his caddying stint, God changed his life, and Ben began following Jesus. He graduated from Dallas Theological Seminary in 2000, earning a ThM degree. He currently serves as the lead pastor of Cypress Community Church in Salinas, California, where he has served since 2010. Ben has worked with Bill on The Bonhoeffer Project since 2015. He is married to Joni. They live in Salinas, California, with their five children.